The
Paterson Strike Pageant

An IWW Novel
of
Bohemia & Insurgent Labor

Eric Leif Davin

DavinBooks
Pittsburgh, Pennsylvania

The Paterson Strike Pageant

An IWW Novel of Bohemia & Insurgent Labor

Copyright 2019 by Eric Leif Davin

All Rights Reserved

ISBN: 978-0-359-89823-7

Back Cover: Pageant Strike Poster by Robert Edmond Jones

Production: Reiko Becker

The
Paterson Strike Pageant

For Larry Evans,
friend, comrade, and troublemaker.

The Republic of Greenwich Village

Greenwich Village lay frozen in darkness and silence. Moonlight bathed the snow-covered Washington Square Park beneath the rebels, and chimney smoke from the residential apartments that ringed the park hung in the clear night air like something solid. It was the last night of 1912, or the first night of 1913. The rebels weren't sure which. None of them, not even John Reed, had brought a watch to the revolution. It didn't matter, Reed thought, as he looked down on the park from his perch atop the Washington Arch. We will proclaim the revolution, no matter what year it was.

Climbing to the top of the Washington Square Arch to ring in the New Year of 1913 was Woe's idea. Her actual name was Gertrude Drick and she had come from somewhere in Texas to study with Ash Can artist John Sloan. However, everyone called her, and she called herself, "Woe." When Reed first met her, he'd asked her why she went by such an odd name. "Because Woe is me," she replied.

Despite that, Woe was anything but woeful. She was renowned for her pranks and stunts, and climbing to the top of the Washington Square Arch to celebrate New Year's Eve was one of them. She had discovered a door in the side of the Washington Arch and a staircase that led to the top. The idea of climbing them and ushering in the New Year atop the Arch immediately popped into her mind, and she began recruiting friends for the party.

Of course, the first person she invited to party with her was her teacher, John Sloan. She had a crush on him. He was married, but so what? This was the Village, after all. Sloan then invited his avant-garde artist friend, Marcel Duchamp. Like Sloan, Duchamp was an artistic rebel who disdained contemporary art. He viewed it as elitist, sterile, and stultifying. He wanted to explode it all in the name of "modernism." So did Sloan, who said he wanted to plant a bomb beneath all convention. But, even though he lauded Cubism and Fauvism, Sloan's rebellion took the form of painting the gritty reality of modern life in a realistic manner, which led critics to label him a painter of lowlifes and "ash cans," thus his style of art came to be called, "Ash Can Art."

Duchamp, on the other hand, felt that such realistic forms were outmoded. They needed to be abandoned, and he had done just that in his most recent painting, "Nude Descending a Staircase." Only the most diligent observer could discern either a nude or a staircase in the rectangular forms in his painting, which was exactly as Duchamp intended. He was going to exhibit the painting in the big show at the New York Armory that was being organized, where he hoped it would create a scandal. Despite their different approaches, however, both Sloan and Duchamp viewed themselves as rebel comrades-in-arms, and so Sloan invited him to the party.

So then Woe invited some of her young actor and actress friends, who were always guaranteed to enliven a party. Then they invited others. The group planning to climb the interior stairs of the Washington Arch in the dark of a December night kept growing. But it was Sloan's idea to also invite John Reed, the Golden Boy of the Village. Reed was not long out of Harvard, but he'd already made a name for himself in the Village as a rabble-rouser, romantic poet, and trouble-making journalist.

And it was Reed's idea to use the occasion to proclaim the independence of the Republic of Greenwich Village, an entity that had nothing in common with the rest of boring bourgeois America, from the highest point in the Village, the top of the Washington Arch. What could be a more appropriate time to do so, than at the start of a brand new year?

The group gathered at Reed's communal apartment at 42 Washington Square South on the other side of the park, which he shared with four classmates from Harvard. Then, laughing and giggling, they trudged through crunchy snow across the park to the Arch. Woe led them to the side door she'd discovered and they stumbled up the dark interior staircase. They soon came out on the top of the Arch into the crisp winter air. A waist-high parapet surrounded the top of the Arch and they rushed to it and gazed out over the park below. The park was peaceful in the moonlight, but it had experienced its share of violence. It was once the scene of public executions and, in 1824, the Marquis de Lafayette, during his famous American tour, was the honored guest at the hanging in the park of some 20 thieves and cutthroats.

"Hello, New York!" Woe called out, and her entourage began hooting and hollering along with her. Then Woe twirled to her friends and cried, "Let's have a picnic!" They'd brought along blankets, bread and cheese, and wine with which to toast the New Year.

"Yes," answered one of her girlfriends, "and let's blow up the balloons!" They'd also brought along red balloons for the festive occasion, and so some of the girls began blowing them up.

"OK," Reed said, "but let's not forget the main reason we came up here." He pulled out several toy cap pistols from his coat pockets and passed along one each to Sloan and Duchamp. "We're here to proclaim the Republic of Greenwich Village!"

"Oh, we'll get your proclamation soon enough," Woe replied. "But first, let's all have some wine and toast the New Year!" Her theater friends greeted the idea with enthusiasm, and one of the men uncorked a wine bottle and began filling the French tumbler glasses they'd brought with them. Reed accepted one along with the others. Then, as they stood in a circle, Woe raised her glass and declared, "Here's to the New Year!" Everyone cheered and threw down a big gulp of wine.

"OK, everyone," Woe cried, "let's tie the balloons to the parapet." The group cheered again and began to tie the balloons along the parapet overlooking the park below. A chill winter wind came up, caught them, and they bobbed wildly back and forth on their tethers.

Then Woe and her girlfriends spread out the blankets and placed the bread and cheese on them, along with the wine bottles and glasses. There was much giggling and joshing as they did so. Woe made sure everyone's tumbler was kept filled.

John Reed enjoyed a good drink and a good party as much as anyone, but he was growing impatient to proclaim the Republic. "OK, before everyone gets too comfortable and too drunk, I want everyone to come join me here by the parapet. We're going to proclaim our independence." Reed had been a cheerleader at Harvard. To Woe, it seemed he couldn't stop being a cheerleader for something or other. Now it was for this independence proclamation he'd thought up.

Sloan and Duchamp quickly joined Reed, with the rest of the party straggling along until they lined the parapet. "Does everyone have a glass of wine?" Reed asked. There was a murmur of assent. "Then here we go."

John Reed held his glass out before him and declaimed to the silent city below:

"In the name of artistic freedom, I hereby proclaim the death of all respectability and convention. In the name of artistic freedom, I hereby proclaim the death of the old world of conformity and morality. And, in the name of artistic freedom, I hereby proclaim the independence of the new world of nonconformity and immorality. I hereby proclaim the independence of the Republic of Greenwich Village!"

The revelers around him whooped at that and the men began firing their toy cap pistols in the air. Then they all gulped down the wine with which they'd toasted the birth of the new republic.

When the cheering died down, John Reed looked around at his fellow rebels. "You know, this is all well and good, but what if there was actually a real revolution with thousands marching in the street? What would you think of that?"

The revelers around him laughed.

"No, I'm serious. What if there was an honest-to-goodness real revolution that kicked the bourgeoisie all to hell. What would you think of that?"

Gertrude Drick held up her wine glass in the cold night air and proclaimed, "Woe is me."

Mabel's Salon

    The black banjo player stomped his foot and strummed his instrument furiously as the black woman swayed and swirled in front of him. "Get down, girl, get down!" he howled. He grinned at the woman, and she grinned back as she grabbed her flowing skirt in both hands and swished it back and forth. She stamped her feet and whooped, and the banjo player yelled, "Thas right, girl, thas right! Get down, get down!"
    Mabel Dodge was mortified. Her face grew hot and feverish, and she glanced around nervously at her guests. Carl Van Vechten was laughing and rocking back and forth as he whooped and hollered along with the performers, clapping his hands in delight. He would, Mabel thought. This was all his idea. He was the music and culture critic for *The New York Times*, and he knew such people. Like so many people in New York, however, Carl was from somewhere else. In his case, it was Cedar Rapids, Iowa. He was fascinated with the spectacle of New York and loved anything that was new and shocking. And it seemed he had accomplished his goal to shock with something new this night. Mabel looked around the room. The rest of her guests, she thought, seemed to stare in either puzzlement or shock or ill-concealed embarrassment.
    This was a bad idea, Mabel decided. I should not have agreed when Carl said he wanted to bring a Negro and Negress from Harlem to sing and dance for us. Mabel looked back at the Negress. Dressed in thigh-high white stockings and high black boots, the woman cavorted before the all-white audience in Mabel's living room. Mabel felt that the woman had singled her out for special attention, and that flustered her. The woman's dancing was wildly abandoned and suggestive. Her skirt seemed to be climbing higher and higher as she moved. And the way the woman leers at me, Mabel thought, it's just too lascivious. Mabel felt hot all over, and then she was cold with fear and alarm at what she had felt. She'd never been so near something as elemental as this. She didn't know what to do.
    And then she calmed herself. "One must just let the Life Force express itself in whatever form it will," she thought. "Let it happen. Let it decide. Let the great force of the universe behind the scenes direct the action. Have faith in it and do not hamper it, or try to shape it." She remembered telling Walter Lippmann, when he complained about the haphazard nature of her gatherings, "I would rather be the leaf in the wind than the wind. *Que sera, sera*. What will be, will be." This had been her philosophy ever since returning from Florence, Italy, a few months before and renting her apartment.
    She could have taken a more expensive apartment in Uptown, but the idea bored her. Instead, she rented this large and pleasant second-floor apartment in a brownstone at 23 Fifth Avenue. It was in the Chelsea neighborhood just north of Washington Square and directly across from the Brevoort Hotel, where almost anything from Europe might be picked up. She wanted to be near Greenwich Village, where she heard that things were happening, but not too close. One could not be sure, after all.
    The building's heavy wooden doors at the top of a small set of concrete steps were of a dark wood with dry and dusty paint. The doorknobs were silver, darkened with age and use. The upper halves of the doors were thick clouded glass with impressive

carved classical figures.

One reached her apartment via dim mahogany red-carpeted stairs climbing past the heavily bolted double doors of fat old General Sickles on the first floor. He was 93-years-old and had lost one of his legs long before in the Civil War. He owned the building, and his dark, heavily curtained apartment was crammed with items of furniture removed from the other apartments in the building after previous tenants left them behind.

Upstairs from Mabel was Governor William Sulzer, Tammany Hall's just-as-reclusive former governor of New York, reputed to be too incompetent even for Tammany Hall. Just before Mabel moved in a Tammany controlled legislature had impeached him. Mabel didn't quite know what "impeachment" meant, but it made the ex-governor seem very mysterious. His wife always referred to him as "The Governor." She had been his housekeeper before he became governor, and she still retained the deference to him acquired during her years of service. The Governor never invited Mabel up to visit him and his wife, and so she had no idea what their apartment looked like.

Mabel knew no one in New York, and so busied herself entirely with making her apartment as pleasing to herself as possible. She covered the gleaming hardwood floors here and there with rich carpets. She draped the eggshell white living room walls with expensive Italian tapestries and silk embroideries from Villa Curonia, her hilltop Renaissance villa in Florence. She loved that Italian villa, where red and gold damask tapestries hung on the walls and peacocks strutted the grounds. Raphael was said to have once lived there. The villa was still hers, but she had grown bored with Florence and thought it might be interesting to return to America, at least for a while. She had never lived in New York City, but had heard about how exciting it had become. Now she was trying to make her new home, her new dwelling, as comfortable as her lovely Villa Curonia.

Bare sections of the apartment's walls displayed many old carved and gilded frames installed with new mirrors, which glinted and sparkled with light. The corner apartment had windows on one side facing East 9th Street, as well as three tall ones facing Fifth Avenue, ensuring that much sunlight streamed in. She graced all the windows with straight, white, hand-woven linen curtains that hung to the floor, and which were drawn at night.

During the day, however, the curtains were tied back so that on sunny afternoons beams of sunlight fell across the room like bands of gold. A large oval table caught the sunlight flickering over gold and white crystal vases filled with fresh-cut flowers and highlighting golden threads in the linen tablespread from Asolo, Italy. Several delicate old gray French chairs, brought from Florence, were placed strategically around the large room. Several *chaise lounges* upholstered in gray-blues and pale yellows, with cushions of old damask and peach-colored brocade and piled with pillows, completed the room.

A Venetian chandelier of white porcelain hung from dark exposed wooden beams of the high ceiling. Its long curving arms were decorated with birds and flowers in canary yellow and turquoise blue. Mabel thought it threw exquisite shadows on her white ceiling after she lit the candles. Also in the evenings, a fire glowed warmly in the room's white marble fireplace, in front of which she placed a huge white bearskin rug from her Florentine villa.

Beyond sliding double doors was the dining room with a large oak table. Next was the kitchen. This was presided over by Mary Malone, a sturdy Irish cook procured by her butler. And past that was the storeroom, filled with cases of wine, white for lunch and red for dinner. The rest of the apartment was the domain of "little Vittorio," her perfectly tailored butler, whom she had brought with her from Florence. In New York, Mabel thought, he looked like a papal emissary. Both Vittorio and Mary lived in an adjacent apartment building on 9th Street with Alberto, Mabel's chauffeur, who kept Mabel's limousine in a basement garage.

Then there was the housekeeper, Miss Galvin, a full-bodied "Hebe," as Mabel called her, who wore her hair in a bun and who did the shopping and kept track of the bills. She also lived in the adjacent apartment building. Each morning Mabel propped herself up on her plump pillows in her pale gray French bed, embraced by gently billowing silk curtains. Miss Galvin then served Mabel coffee in a delicate porcelain cup with a small porcelain cream pitcher and porcelain sugar bowl, all on a silver tray.

Mabel's bed, imported from Paris, had a canopy from which four white silk curtains hung, drawn back at each corner. Her wide bed in Villa Curonia had been all white, and she replicated that bed here in her new home. Behind the headboard Mabel had hung a glimmering white embroidered shawl. At the windows of the bedroom, looking out on East 9th Street, were more yards and yards of white silk. The room dazzled the eye with all the white on white.

But nothing lifted Mabel's spirits. She sipped her coffee and studied the pale clouds of cream swirling in her cup. Then she gazed at the room around her and sighed with great weariness and boredom. Mabel knew no one in the city and had nothing to look forward to for the rest of the day. She simply drifted through her beautiful, silent apartment filled with Italian antiques. At half past one on a gloriously sunny Saturday afternoon she would sit in her living room smoking her Curtis cigarettes, kept by the hundreds in a green glass bowl on the oval table with the Asolo linen tablespread. She smoked and stared out at the busy life below her on Fifth Avenue. "Nothing to do, yet again," Mabel thought. "I'm alone, and to be alone is to be nothing. It's all so depressing." Mabel was just entering her thirties and thought of herself as a mysterious and alluring *femme fatale*, but it was hard to be a *femme fatale* if there was no one to lure.

That was when Hutchins Hapgood suggested the "Evenings." Hutch was an acquaintance of Gertrude Stein's, whom Mabel knew from Florence. When Stein learned that Mabel knew no one in New York, she suggested Hutch. He was a well-connected journalist and knew everyone in New York who was worth knowing. Mabel soon became close friends with Hutch and his wife, Neith Boyce. Neith was named after an ancient Egyptian goddess and, like many of the "Modern Women," retained her maiden name. She seemed exotic, and even alluring, to Mabel.

"You have this beautiful large apartment," Hutch said one day after Mabel complained of her loneliness. "Why don't I invite some of my friends over and you can get to know them?"

"You mean for dinner?" Mabel asked. "I wouldn't know what to say."

"No, nothing as formal as that. Just for conversation."

That she would be expected to make witty conversation with Hutch's friends terrified her. She thought of herself as forgetful and muddle-headed, and intellectual conversation bored her. "I don't know," she said doubtfully.

"Don't worry," Hutch said, grasping her fear. "You wouldn't have to say anything. They all have more than enough to say, and are eager to say it. You could just listen to them arguing with each other. You'd enjoy it, and you'd get to know people, important people."

Mabel liked the sound of that. She turned the idea over in her mind, savoring it.

She liked to know important people. She liked to know the heads of things, the heads of newspapers and magazines, the heads of groups and movements, people who stood out above the common herd. She had a fierce longing to be part of a group, but not an ordinary group. She wanted to belong to a group of witty, important people, people she could collect and arrange about herself like the flowers in the crystal vases that filled her apartment. This was how it had been in Florence. It was how she had gotten to know Gertrude Stein. Now Hutch could be her entrée to such people in New York.

"Yes," she finally said. "I think I would like that."

And so the Evenings began, filling a void in Mabel's life and enabling her to meet people, which she so desperately wanted to do. In Florence, she had known everyone worth knowing. Here she knew no one. Now, once a week, strangers, but all people known to Hutch, filled her elegant living room for "discussions." These were not speeches, but discussions, on any conceivable topic. Sometimes, as the artists and writers, the businessmen and radicals, the sculptors and painters, the suffragists and journalists mixed and mingled and laughed, there was no topic at all. Sometimes the talk was brilliant and illuminating, as when anarchists who believed in "Direct Action" argued with socialists, who believed that legislation was the way to utopia. Sometimes, however, as arguments floated in the air, the talk simply was riotous and foolish. And always Mabel felt the tense undercurrent of erotic attraction between the men and the "Modern Women" like Neith Boyce, boldly smoking Mabel's Curtis cigarettes that filled exquisite glass bowls scattered around her apartment.

At midnight Vittorio would throw open the sliding double doors dividing the living room from the dining room. There, revealed on the oak table, was sliced ham and turkey; cheeses of various exotic kinds that Mary Malone had prepared, along with bottles of expensive red wine. Her guests fell upon the feast, and the discussions became even more raucous as they ate and drank, laughing and flirting with each other. Mabel felt a *frisson* of excitement at the undercurrent of sexual tension in these gatherings, and sometimes felt drawn to this person or that, and yet she never acted overtly on such impulses. Instead, she waited silently, patiently, trusting in her innate animal magnetism to draw people to her.

Nor did Mabel ever take part in the discussions. Sometimes she hardly even knew what the scintillating speakers were saying. She merely sat or stood in the background and smiled silently and enigmatically, with a look of understanding on her face. As the fascinating people flowed up the mahogany stairs and into her home, she stood apart, aloof and withdrawn, dressed in a long, white, flowing silk gown, with perhaps an emerald chiffon scarf wrapped around her neck. She never uttered a word beyond a remote, "How do you do?" As her guests left she would give each one her hand and, with a small smile, impersonal and remote, she murmured, "I hope you will come again if you enjoyed the evening."

And so Mabel gained a reputation as a wise sphinx with "a Mona Lisa smile," an enigma to all her guests. Her facility for saying very little, yet for being there, remote from all that swirled around her, gave people's imaginations a chance to fabricate their own "Mable Dodge." Mabel facilitated their imaginations and enhanced her mystery by giving selected guests copies of Gertrude Stein's "Portrait of Mabel Dodge at the Villa Curonia," written in Stein's elusive and incomprehensible style. Stein and her lover, Alice Toklas, had stayed as Mabel's guests for two weeks in Florence, on their way back from Spain to Paris. Stein had fallen in love with the villa. She wrote the "Portrait," one of a series of such portraits of people she knew, to celebrate both the villa, and the woman who owned it.

And Mabel had fallen in love with Stein's flattering portrait of her. She quickly arranged to have 300 copies printed in a small booklet form, bound in beautiful wrappers of flowered wallpaper. She had brought these booklets with her from Italy, and now she gave them out strategically to her guests as they left. She made especially sure she gave copies to newspaper or magazine editors, or influential journalists such as Carl Van Vechten. No one in America knew who Gertrude Stein was, but Stein's disconnected language, pushed to hermetic lengths, intrigued them, and so the booklet helped to also make Mabel intriguing and mysterious to them.

Thus, they attributed to her all kinds of faculties and powers she did not possess. She was reputed to be radical and emancipated and daring, but in reality she was none of that. She was merely a leaf in the wind, blown hither and yon, willing to be taken wherever the wind carried her.

And so when Carl suggested a "Harlem Evening," with a musician and a dancer he knew, she agreed. Now, as the black seductress danced suggestively before her, and the banjo player yelled "Get down, girl, get down!" she wondered if, for once, the evening had truly gotten out of hand. She felt as if the woman were leering lustily directly at her, and she felt herself burning all over and her breathing quickened. She looked furtively around at her guests, wondering if anybody noticed her discomfort.

But no one was looking at her; no one noticed. All attention was focused on the black woman dancing before them.

And so Mabel Dodge smiled her enigmatic smile, and nodded knowingly at the dancing woman, as if she knew exactly what the woman was suggesting.

Duchamp's Nude

Mabel Dodge sat patiently in Marcel Duchamp's atelier, listening to the artist talk about himself. Men enjoyed talking about themselves and their accomplishments in Mabel's placid presence. She was a receptive listener, seldom interrupting. She just smiled her enigmatic smile and nodded, as if she was peering into their deepest souls and understood everything they were saying. This encouraged them to say more, perhaps more than they intended. Duchamp was no exception. Haughty and sure of himself, he accepted such attention as his due, and so he rambled on, explaining his most recent painting on the easel in front of him.

Mabel glanced around the cramped studio, crowded with Duchamp's paintings leaning in files against the walls. At the front of one of the files was his "Nude Descending A Staircase." She had come to visit the immigrant Frenchman because she was told he would be exhibiting that particular painting in the upcoming Armory Show. Mabel liked to know important people, people who were being talked about, people who mattered. Duchamp was one of those who mattered, and so she was here.

And there was the painting. It was like nothing she'd seen, but, then, that was the whole point of "modern art," was it not? It was new, inexplicable, mysterious, revolutionary. The whole purpose of "modern art" was to defy conventions. Duchamp chattered on about his ideas on art as she stared at the painting. He did not notice that her attention had wandered from him. Where, she wondered, was the nude in the painting? All she saw was sharp rectangular angles superimposed on each other in a continuous series, perhaps descending a staircase. Mostly, though, it was simply incomprehensible to her, as were so many of the modernist paintings to be exhibited in the upcoming Armory Show.

That, however, had not stopped Mabel from throwing herself into preparations for the Armory Show, once she was invited to do so. Mabel loved being involved in anything important that was happening. But, it was all serendipity. Mabel felt she was merely a leaf in the wind, and had simply proven to be in the right place at the right time, and had gotten to know the right people. One of those people was F. J. Gregg, a newspaperman hired to do publicity for the Armory Show.

Gregg had attended one of Mabel's "Evenings" at her "salon," as everyone was now calling them. Mabel had made sure she pressed a copy of Gertrude Stein's "Portrait of Mabel Dodge at the Villa Curonia" into his hand as he left. Gregg was pleased at his good luck in discovering Mabel's connection to Stein. Several of the gallery dealers who were organizing the Show had visited the Paris apartment of Stein and her brother, Leo. Paintings by Picasso, Matisse, and other of the new so-called "Cubist" artists who were friends with the Steins covered the apartment walls. The dealers arranged to borrow the paintings from the Steins for the Show. Now, here was a person right here in New York who knew Gertrude Stein, and she could introduce the Show's patroness to an American audience.

So Gregg asked Mabel to write an article about Stein and her new style of writing for the prestigious *Arts and Decoration* magazine. The magazine was planning to devote its entire March, 1913, issue to the Armory Show. The issue would go on sale shortly after the Show opened on February 17th. In addition, as a complement to the exhibition, plenty of extra copies would be available at the Show itself throughout its run to March 15th. An article about the unknown Stein and her new revolutionary style of writing would be a perfect inclusion.

Mabel was frightened by the idea. What could she possibly say about Gertrude Stein's Delphic writing style? She could not possibly convey the essence of Stein's writing. But, it was a great opportunity to spread Mabel's own legend, and so she agreed. She entitled her essay, written in a sober and deliberate style, "Speculations, or Post-Impressionism in Prose." In it she claimed that Gertrude Stein was pioneering an entirely new, modernist, form of prose that would do for literature what the paintings of Picasso and Matisse were doing for the world of painting. With Stein, Mabel wrote, "Every word lives, like a kind of sensuous music. Listening to Stein's words and forgetting to try to understand what they mean, one submits to their gradual charm." Gertrude Stein, she said, "is finding the hidden and inner nature of Nature." Mabel wasn't sure she, herself, knew what she meant by that, but it sounded good.

Then, committed to the success of the Armory Show, Mabel donated $200 to the costs of the exhibit and persuaded her wealthy mother back home in Buffalo, New York, to donate a further $500. In gratitude, the organizers made Mabel a vice president of the exhibition's board of directors.

Following that, Carl Van Vechten interviewed Mabel for an article he was writing on her and Gertrude Stein for his paper, *The New York Times*. With the headline, "Cubist of Letters Writes A New Book," it was scheduled to appear in the paper on February 17th, the very day the Armory Show opened. It would be great publicity. At the same time the Armory Show introduced modern art to America, it would also make the name of the completely unknown Gertrude Stein famous. Privately, to herself, Mabel also felt that her own name would thereby become famous. In a short time, Mabel was becoming an influential, or at least a well-known, member of the city's cultural *avant-garde*. It was a warm and pleasant feeling. Mabel wrote an excited letter to her "Cubist of Letters" friend back in Paris about all of the Armory Show's publicity. "This will be a *scream!*" she wrote Stein. "There will be a riot and a revolution and things will never be quite the same afterwards."

But she still felt she did not quite understand the meaning of the paintings with which she was associating herself and Gertrude Stein. Perhaps it would be wise to learn a little more, so that she could speak somewhat knowledgeably about them. Mabel cleared her throat and said, "Pardon moi, Monsieur Duchamp."

Startled, for Mabel seldom spoke, Duchamp turned from the painting on his easel and looked at her, as if he had forgotten that she was in the room. "Oui, madam?"

Mabel gestured at the puzzling painting. "Your 'Nude Descending A Staircase.' It will be in the Armory Show, will it not?"

Duchamp paused, his palette in his left hand and his brush held delicately aloft in his right. He turned in the direction of Mabel's gaze. "Oui, madam. And it will startle and amaze all who see it. Those fools in Paris rejected it last year for their exhibit at the *Section d'Or*. They know nothing, and did not deserve to have it in their exhibition. Now they will discover the error of their ways. It will shock the bourgeoisie and be talk of the show."

Mabel nodded, as if in agreement. That, after all, was what people were saying. If all the connoisseurs said so, it must be so. "I'm sure you are correct, Monsieur Duchamp.

It is a masterpiece. And, of course, a painting speaks for itself. But, I wonder if you would indulge me and tell me a little about how you came to paint it?"

Duchamp smiled, more than ready to talk about his work to an appreciative woman. "Of course, madam."

He set down his brush and palette and wiped his hands on his paint-splattered smock. Mabel thought that Joseph's coat of many colors might have looked somewhat like Duchamp's smock. He picked up a dirty rag and wiped his hands more thoroughly with it. As he did so he studied the painting about which Mabel asked. "An artist does not like to talk about his work, of course," Duchamp said, which, in his case, was not true at all.

"Of course," Mabel replied. "I understand. But if you would indulge me?"

Duchamp smiled at her and cleared his throat. "You are familiar, of course, with the photographic work of Eadweard Muybridge?"

Mabel was not, but she nodded knowingly and replied, "Of course."

Duchamp continued on, as if he had not heard her. "This is an artistic articulation of his work, an abstraction at an elevated level, if you will."

Mabel nodded. "Go on."

Duchamp hardly needed the encouragement, and plunged on. "In 1878 Muybridge took up the challenge of answering a simple question: Does a galloping horse ever have all four feet off the ground at any one moment? The answer is not obvious, for a galloping horse is too fast for the human eye to definitively answer the question.

"Muybridge, however, realized that the newly invented camera could answer the question. But, in order to freeze the motion of the galloping horse, he would have to use a series of cameras. And so he set up a line of cameras triggered by a timing device, each camera timed to go off a fraction of a second after the previous one. After a number of attempts, he was successful in proving in a series of photographs that a galloping horse does, indeed, lift all four feet off the ground during part of its stride."

"Yes, of course," Mabel murmured. "And that series of photographs was the inspiration for your painting?"

"Not directly," Duchamp replied. "All Muybridge did was record what was there. But then one of my countrymen, a physiologist named Marey, saw the possibilities of his photographs to record and analyze motion itself, in all its dimensions. Marey wanted to study the positions of key parts of the body, such as bones and joints. Therefore, he dressed models head to toe in black, with white lines painted on the suits to represent bones and white dots at the joints. Then he photographed his models moving against black backgrounds, so that they looked like disembodied stick figures, abstractions of human bodies."

"Ah," said Mabel. "And so that inspired this work."

Duchamp smiled tolerantly at Mabel. "Not yet. Then another countryman, Paul Richer, also a physiologist, realized that Marey's photographs could be used to analyze the specific physical dynamics of human motion. He traced Marey's photographs to determine the center of gravity of the motions, and so forth. Bodies became masses; bones and joints became levers; motion became a mere function of force and velocity. We could thus understand human physical motion, but how could it be portrayed on a static canvas, instead of in a photograph? Ah, that was the problem! And I, of course, solved the problem, as you can see."

Mabel disliked all forms of machinery, so cold and alien, and Duchamp's talk of the human body in motion as a mere machine in motion did not appeal to her. But she smiled, concealing her distaste. "Yes," she said, nodding wisely, "I can see."

Duchamp cleared his throat uncomfortably. He realized, belatedly, that he had revealed far too much about his painting. "Madam, you have a facility for making men reveal themselves. An artist should cultivate an air of mystery. He should not explain too much. If the sources upon which the artist draws are unknown to the viewer, a painting such as mine appears mysterious and incomprehensible, as it should be. Once the sources and context are known, however, such a painting not only makes sense, it becomes an inevitable evolution. Best that the viewer never knows from whence comes inspiration. Thus, like 'Nude Descending A Staircase,' it remains a revolutionary mystery."

"Yes," Mabel agreed, "I'm sure the viewers at the Show will find it a truly revolutionary mystery."

Duchamp smiled at that, and turned to gaze upon his painting with renewed pride.

But, to Mabel, the painting still seemed incomprehensible and no less mysterious, despite Duchamp's explanation of its inspiration. It remained a puzzle to her. Where, exactly, she wondered, was the nude?

When Carlo Met Gurley

Elizabeth Gurley Flynn felt the tension rising in Carlo Tresca as he sat next to her in the audience. Jacob Panken, the Socialist Party speaker on the platform, had been rambling on about how the angry workers gathered in the hall should just be patient and take out their frustrations at the polls. Vote for the Socialist Party at the next election, Panken told them, and if the Socialists won, they would see that the workers were justly treated. Elizabeth hadn't been with Carlo very long, but she knew him well enough to know that he wouldn't be able to contain his mounting irritation at such nonsense much longer. He was going to erupt any moment.

Elizabeth first met Carlo when he came to Lawrence, Massachusetts, the previous year. He had come to lead the agitation surrounding the trial of Joe Ettor and Arturo Giovannitti. They had been the initial organizers that the IWW, the Industrial Workers of the World, had sent to Lawrence to help the striking textile workers there. During a street fight between the police and the workers, the police killed a woman picket. No policeman was charged with the woman's death. However, through some elaborate theory of conspiracy, the police arrested Ettor and Giovannitti as accessories to the woman's murder because they had given speeches urging picketing.

Elizabeth, already a well-respected IWW organizer, and Wobbly leader Big Bill Haywood then went to Lawrence to replace Ettor and Giovannitti. And, although Ettor and Giovannitti spent the rest of the strike in jail awaiting trial, the strike ended after two months with a great victory for the workers and the IWW.

But the two Wobblies remained in jail awaiting trial for murder. The IWW, however, did not abandon jailed comrades. Their motto was that of the Three Musketeers, "One for all and all for one." They immediately began agitating for the release of Ettor and Giovannitti.

Since Italian immigrants made up a big part of the Lawrence workforce, the IWW asked around for a native Italian speaker to lead the campaign. Everyone suggested Carlo Tresca. He was an anarchist immigrant from Southern Italy who had fled his native country to escape imprisonment there. He was no less troublesome in America. He became a leader of Italian workers in the Pittsburgh region and made a lot of coal company enemies in the Western Pennsylvania coalfields. Indeed, he carried a scar on his neck from where a hired assassin had tried to cut his throat.

But that didn't silence Carlo Tresca. He was a big tough man, as big in bulk almost as Big Bill Haywood himself, and just as fearless. His name was legendary among Italian immigrants, and he was the obvious choice to lead the agitation for Ettor and Giovannitti. Besides, he was a friend of Giovannitti's and he knew Joe Ettor from when Ettor had helped lead the successful 1909 IWW strike at the Pressed Steel Car Company in McKees Rocks, just outside Pittsburgh.

At the time Tresca was editing an anarcho-syndicalist Italian-language newspaper in New Kensington, near Pittsburgh. He'd just gotten out of jail in the nearby town of Blawnox himself, where he served a term for a supposedly libelous article attacking a local Western Pennsylvania politician. Of course, Carlo Tresca went to Lawrence when he received the call.

Elizabeth met him for the first time when he arrived in Lawrence on May Day, 1912. Elizabeth, who everyone called "Gurley," was from New York City, with dark hair and sad blue eyes. Raised in an Irish socialist family, she read *The Communist Manifesto* in 1906 at age 15 and joined the IWW the same year, just one year after its founding. Also at 15 she gave her first speech at a political gathering, "What Socialism Will Do For Women." It was a huge success, and she quickly became a popular speaker who was in much demand for both her rabble-rousing eloquence and for the novelty of her being intelligent, pretty, and still a teenage girl. Journalist Theodore Dreiser described her that year as "An East Side Joan of Arc" that the capitalist world had better take seriously. By age 16 she was traveling the country as a paid IWW "jawsmith," as they called their speakers.

Thus, when Carlo Tresca first saw Elizabeth on a street in Lawrence, she was still only 21, but already a veteran IWW organizer. He was instantly attracted to her. Carlo's English was still rudimentary, but from the moment he saw her he made it clear he wanted her. Carlo was tall and handsome and in his mid-thirties, with a moustache and a well-trimmed Van Dyke beard, and with his own reputation as a resourceful and dangerous troublemaker. Elizabeth reciprocated his feelings.

Carlo expressed his love by giving Elizabeth a copy of Gabriele D'Annunzio's *The Maidens of the Rocks*. In it he wrote, "Suppose at some time you read this book some flame is kindled in your heart – remember at this time *mio dolce cuore*, my sweetheart, dream, hope, light of my soul – one heart has the same flame for you alone."

Elizabeth responded by giving Carlo a copy of Elizabeth Barrett Browning's *Sonnets from the Portuguese*. She inscribed it "From Elizabeth to Carlo," with appropriate and meaningful passages of the love poems underlined. Carlo put it in the inside breast pocket of his suit coat and carried it with him always. From time to time he took it out and studied the underlined passages, teasing out their words in the English language he was still learning.

Carlo was a resourceful organizer whose favorite English expression was "I fix!" He quickly took charge of the agitation surrounding the trial of the Wobbly organizers. The police tried to arrest him during one protest march, but the attempt resulted in a melee during which the marchers injured two policemen. The Lawrence police didn't try to arrest him again. In September, 1912, the workers shut down every mill in the city demanding the release of the jailed Wobblies. As a result, their trial was moved to nearby Salem. There, just before Thanksgiving, a perhaps less biased jury acquitted the men of all conspiracy charges. They made a triumphant return to Lawrence, where they were greeted at the train station by thousands of cheering workers.

Afterward, Elizabeth returned to the home of her extended family in New York's South Bronx. Not long after, Carlo transferred his newspaper from New Kensington to New York. With his charm, humor, and culinary talents, he quickly ingratiated himself with Elizabeth's parents and her sisters. They accepted him into their home and he became one of the family.

Almost immediately Carlo and Elizabeth were caught up in the agitation surrounding the effort of an independent union trying to organize the waiters, cooks, and kitchen help at New York's fanciest hotels. Many of the hotel workers were Italian immigrants and, when they asked the IWW for help, the Wobblies sent Carlo Tresca and Elizabeth Gurley Flynn.

The culinary workers held their organizing meetings at a large facility known as

Bryant Hall, on Sixth Avenue and 42nd Street. At a mass meeting on January 24th, 1913, thousands of angry workers gathered to decide whether or not to call a general strike against every big hotel in Manhattan. Jacob Panken, a prominent Socialist attorney who was serving as legal counsel for the union, was the featured speaker at the meeting. He mounted the platform and, with his deep voice and florid oratory, urged caution. A strike was not a good idea, Panken said. Instead, take your grievances to the polls and vote for Socialist candidates. Once elected, they will take care of you.

Panken was a hero to the immigrant socialist Jewish workers of the Lower East Side, but was not such a great hero to the mostly Italian hotel workers in the hall. They had immediate problems: low pay, ill treatment, and miserable working conditions. They couldn't wait for a sweet socialist bye-and-bye. They wanted action, and they wanted it now. A murmur of grumbling dissent rippled through the gathering.

Carlo Tresca sensed the discontent of the workers, and Elizabeth sensed Carlo's increasing irritation at Panken's words. She shared his disgust with Panken and his panacea of the polls. Neither Carlo nor Elizabeth had any use for caution and elections. Carlo was an anarchist, who believed in nothing but "direct action," and Elizabeth was a syndicalist, who believed in the union, not in any political party, not even a socialist one.

Finally, Carlo lost patience. He rose from his seat next to Elizabeth and climbed up in his chair. Panken had a strong and loud voice, but Carlo's booming basso was stronger and louder. "Fellow workers!" he shouted. Silence fell in the hall, and even Panken stopped in mid-sentence, as all heads turned in Carlo's direction. "A strike," Carlo boomed, "a strike is not a course of lectures. It is a fight! Dis man, he talk about politics, he talk about elections, while scabs betray our cause! I say we stop talking! I say we act! I say we march in mass formation right now out of here and picket all hotels! I say we win dis strike! Who is with me?"

The hall erupted in cheers and raised fists. Carlo jumped down from his chair and headed for the door, with Elizabeth by his side. The angry workers surged after them. They all poured out of the hall, ready to do battle.

Outside a phalanx of police armed with clubs awaited them. The workers plunged into the massed police, with Carlo Tresca and Elizabeth Gurley Flynn in the lead. The two sides merged in a chaos of fists and flailing clubs. A police club sent Elizabeth reeling and Carlo was beaten to the pavement. A mass of policemen surrounded Carlo, bleeding on the pavement, and sent Elizabeth and the workers falling back. The police hauled Carlo up and threw him and a number of the hotel workers into the back of a nearby police wagon. Elizabeth watched in fury and frustration as the wagon hurtled away.

Carlo and the arrested workers were released from jail the next morning. Elizabeth was waiting for him as he came out of the jail. She had the morning newspaper with her. Carlo's coat and vest had been torn from him during the melee and the contents of their pockets scattered. Among the contents was Carlo's *Sonnets from the Portuguese* that Elizabeth had given him. Someone had picked it up and recognized their names inside. He had immediately taken it to *The New York Times*, and the paper ran with it. There, on the front page, in a story about the hotel workers' "riot", were photos of both Elizabeth and Carlo. There were also photos of the book cover, Elizabeth's dedication of the book to Carlo, and photos of the underlined sonnets. The newspaper whooped with delight about the revelation of a "hidden IWW romance." It was all so embarrassing.

"I'm so sorry, Carlo," she said as he glanced over the photos.

Carlo handed the newspaper back to her and smiled. "Do not be sorry," he said.

"Let the whole world know that we love each other! What do we care?"
 Then he bent over her, grasped her tightly, and kissed her fiercely on her lips.

Love and Anarchy

Carlo Tresca was too much of an anarchist to join an organization even as decentralized as the IWW. He was willing to work with the Wobblies, and work hard. He would answer their call for help with strikes, and go where they asked him to go. He believed in strikes, but not because they might win any material gains for workers. He believed that strikes, even lost strikes, served a positive purpose by helping to develop militancy and a revolutionary consciousness among striking workers. This was even more important, he believed, than victory. So, he was willing to work with the IWW during strikes. But he would not become a member of the IWW.

This bothered Elizabeth Gurley Flynn. It was good, she felt, that Carlo rejected the Socialist Party's belief in elections as the road to victory. She agreed with him on that. Her own father was a party member and a committed Socialist who read everything by Marx and Engels he could get his hands on. He even ran for the state legislature as a Socialist Party candidate.

But Elizabeth, as a dedicated Wob, had no faith at all in her father's brand of socialism. When Carlo and her father sat at the family's kitchen table and argued loudly into the night over politics and elections, strikes and revolution, she always sided with Carlo in his rejection of her father's faith that elections, and only elections, would eventually bring about the workers' paradise.

But she had problems with Carlo's anarchist rejection of working class organization. Elizabeth was committed to the IWW's belief in the "One Big Union." Those inclined to theoretical terminology called this idea "syndicalism," after the French word "syndicate," their word for a labor union. What the Wobblies wanted to do was organize all workers, and not just American workers, into One Big Union. That was why the IWW was called the Industrial Workers...*of the World*.

Then, when all the workers of the world, regardless of job description or industry or nationality, were organized into One Big Union, they would call a worldwide general strike. The world economy would grind to a halt and capitalism would collapse. The One Big Union would then take control of the world economy and run it for the benefit of all working people. That would be the revolution. That was how socialism would be won, not through her father's elections.

But the anarchists seemed to reject even this kind of syndicalist organization. They seemed to just believe in simple agitation and, when enough workers were agitated enough, they would spontaneously rise in violent revolution and overthrow world capitalism. They didn't need organization into any One Big Union to accomplish this. It would simply...*happen*.

Elizabeth could never go along with this. So, just as she rejected elections, she also rejected the anarchist idea of a spontaneous violent revolution, as well as their belief in assassinations. It seemed the anarchists, like the Russian Nihilists before them who killed Czar Alexander, were always willing to kill someone for the revolution. In 1900 an Italian anarchist from Paterson, New Jersey, a hotbed of immigrant Italian anarchism, went back to Italy and killed King Umberto I. In 1901, a Polish anarchist immigrant named Leon Czolgosz, known to the famous anarchist Emma Goldman, killed American President William McKinley. Emma Goldman had also conspired with her lover, Alexander Berkman, to assassinate steel baron Henry Clay Frick during the famous steel lockout and strike at Homestead, Pennsylvania, just outside Pittsburgh. Berkman had failed in that attempt, but not for lack of trying. Elizabeth couldn't go along with any of this.

Nor could she go along with the anarchist idea of "free love." Elizabeth and her family were Irish, and her mother still spoke with the thick Irish brogue of her native Ireland. But they were not Catholic. Being socialists, they were "unchurched," and had nothing to do with pulpits and priests. Even so, her parents still believed in marriage and were married. And Elizabeth, also, believed in marriage.

This was a problem she had with Emma Goldman and the whole bohemian crowd in Greenwich Village, where Goldman lived. The world of New York City radicalism was a small one, and everyone seemed to know everyone. So, when Elizabeth became a local celebrity shortly after her debut speech, she quickly got to know everyone. One of the people she soon met was Goldman, who lived just west of Washington Square in an apartment above a bohemian café called the Purple Pup.

Goldman then introduced Elizabeth to her lover, Alexander Berkman, at a "welcome home" party she threw for him after his release from prison in Pittsburgh. Berkman surprised Elizabeth as much as had Goldman. Belying her radical reputation, Elizabeth found the short, stout, and plainly dressed Goldman to resemble a kindly and motherly matron more than the expected dangerous and fiery-eyed revolutionary. Likewise, she found would-be assassin Alexander Berkman to be gentle and courteous.

Everyone knew about Berkman's attempt on Frick's life. Back in 1892, the ironworkers in Homestead had fought a violent strike against Andrew Carnegie and his partner, Henry Clay Frick. Carnegie and Frick sent a 300-man private army of Pinkertons to Homestead to break the strike. The workers, however, fought and defeated the Pinkerton army, forcing it to surrender. It looked to many radicals like the country was on the verge of revolution, and all that was needed was a climactic violent act to push it over the edge. Goldman and Berkman decided that violent act had to be the assassination of Frick.

So, Goldman helped Berkman buy a pistol and a train ticket to Pittsburgh. There, Berkman barged into Frick's downtown Pittsburgh office and shot and stabbed him. Fortunately, or unfortunately, he did not kill Frick. However, he certainly helped kill the Homestead strike. Public opinion, previously favorable to the workers, turned against them and the governor sent in the militia to break the strike. Berkman himself was sentenced to 13 years in prison for attempted murder.

During the years Berkman was in the Western Pennsylvania Penitentiary outside Pittsburgh, Goldman remained faithful to the anarchist ideal they both shared. She continued speaking and agitating. However, she did not remain faithful to Berkman. In 1899 she went to London, where she visited the people of the abyss in Whitechapel and the East End. There she met a wild-eyed and wild-haired Czech anarchist named Hippolyte Havel. He had fled Austria-Hungary, where the authorities sought him for his revolutionary activities. They became lovers, and Goldman took Havel along with her to Paris, where she attended an international anarchist convention. Then, when she returned to New York, she brought her new lover back home with her to America. Once ensconced in Greenwich Village, Hippolyte Havel quickly became a well-known figure in the bohemian community, where everyone called him "Hippie" Havel.

When Goldman and Hippie Havel grew tired of each other, Hippie took up with another anarchist woman of the Village named Polly Holladay, who also believed in "free love." Polly, like so many others, had come to the Village from elsewhere, in her case that being Evanston, Illinois. She opened a restaurant, simply called "Polly's," at 137 Macdougal Street, just outside Washington Square. On the floor above it was the Liberal Club, where all the assorted radicals of the Village assembled for their "Pagan Revels" and to listen to speeches from the *avant-garde* thinkers of the day. As well as her lover, Hippie Havel became Polly's cook and waiter. All the bohemians of the Village went to Polly's, where one could get a good and filling meal for 35-cents, and where Hippie Havel reviled them all as "bourgeois pigs," his favorite epithet, as he served them.

Alexander Berkman, when he came home from his Pennsylvania prison, did not blame Emma Goldman for her love affair with Hippie Havel while he was in prison. He believed in "free love" as much as did Goldman and, in fact, he became friends with Hippie Havel. They often drank together at Hippie's favorite Village bar, the Hell Hole, where Hippie was known for his drunken and obscene ravings against the bourgeoisie more than for any coherent radical discussion.

Elizabeth remembered meeting Hippie Havel in 1906, when she was 15 and was just becoming known as a radical "girl speaker." Big Bill Haywood, then a leader of the Western Federation of Miners, was awaiting trial in Idaho on the charge of assassinating former Governor Frank Steunenberg for his anti-labor actions during a strike. Everyone knew it was a frame-up and that Big Bill was innocent, and so there were protest meetings everywhere demanding his release. Elizabeth was invited to speak in favor of his release at a big Socialist Party rally at the Cooper Union in Union Square. To celebrate the invitation, Berkman offered to treat the novice girl speaker to an expensive dinner at Luchow's, the famous German restaurant on 14th Street. Hippie Havel, drunk as usual, invited himself along to meet the girl celebrity.

Elizabeth did not find him appealing. The small, bespeckled, wild-haired Czech anarchist was disheveled and drunkenly aggressive in his attentions toward her. He kept kissing Elizabeth's hand and telling the teenager how beautiful she was. Elizabeth knew that Hippie Havel had a reputation for telling every woman he met she was beautiful, especially when he was drunk. Elizabeth was not flattered. Rather, she was embarrassed by his attentions. Berkman, aware of her embarrassment, kept kicking Hippie Havel under the table, telling him to behave himself and leave Elizabeth alone.

"What the hell's the matter with you, Sasha?" Hippie Havel complained. "Why are you kicking me? I'm not doing anything!" Then Hippie Havel returned to telling Elizabeth how beautiful she was, while slobbering over her hand. And Berkman kicked him again, and again told him to leave her alone.

It was certainly an unpleasant experience for the teenage Elizabeth, but she also could hardly contain her puzzlement that the two anarchists were friends at all. She knew that both of them had been Emma Goldman's lovers. But, instead of being angry with Hippie Havel for taking up with Goldman while he was in prison, the gentle and courteous Berkman was friends with him. Elizabeth could not understand that at all. She certainly would not have been a friend with any rival for Carlo's attentions.

They finally escaped Hippie Havel and Berkman safely escorted Elizabeth to the rally at the Cooper Union for her speaking engagement. However, as soon as the two of them walked into the hall together, with Elizabeth holding onto Berkman's arm, the Socialists in the crowd became agitated. They surrounded Elizabeth's mother, there to hear Elizabeth speak, and warned her that she should never let her teenage daughter be seen in the company of such a dangerous anarchist and would-be assassin as Alexander Berkman.

But, Elizabeth thought, it was anarchist Hippie Havel that they should really be warning her mother against, dangerous in an entirely different way than Alexander Berkman.

So, there were many things about both love and anarchy that Elizabeth did not understand, nor agree with. She and Carlo often argued, long and loud, about such things.

And then they resolved their differences in bed.

A Cold Day in the Silk City

January 27th was a cold and dark day in Paterson, New Jersey. The sun was not yet up as Max Gerstein entered the big Henry Doherty silk mill where he worked. It was the start of another tedious ten-hour day. It had snowed overnight and a white blanket of snow, turning to dirty slush, covered all the streets. Max, a broad-silk weaver, started up the two silk looms before him. All around him other weavers on his shift were doing the same. All told, there were almost a thousand weavers employed in the Doherty mill. Each weaver tended two power looms and, once they got their looms going, the noise was deafening.

Starting the looms took the most time and skill. A weaver had to set all the threads so they wove smoothly. After that it became a job of watching the looms closely, tending them, making sure the silk threads didn't tangle and break. As a batch of silk ran out, the weaver had to slide the same class of silk thread smoothly into the loom on one side as the woven and finished silk came out on the other side. A silk weaver's skill was in his eyes and hands, seeing and feeling the flow of the silk threads as the loom wove them together. You couldn't be a greenhorn fresh off the boat and just walk into a mill and tend the looms. It took years to learn how to do it properly, and most weavers started in the mills as children, learning the skill from their fathers.

That was the way it had been with Max. His father had been a silk weaver in Bialystok, Russian Poland, where Max was born. Max did have some years of schooling. However, when he turned ten his father took him into the mill with him and taught him how to weave silk. He had been doing it ever since. His time in the Bialystok mills was interrupted when he participated in the 1905 revolution against the czar. The revolution was brutally suppressed and, like thousands of others, Max was sentenced to exile in Siberia. He escaped, but he couldn't return to Bialystok. So, like many other Polish Jews, he fled to America. And, like many other skilled immigrant silk weavers, he wound up in Paterson, the silk capitol of America.

Paterson was about 15 miles northwest of New York City. Alexander Hamilton had seen the industrial potential of the site long before. The Passaic River flows down from the New Jersey uplands, through the heart of Paterson, and then over the swirling Great Falls. It crashes down into a misty abyss, creating the largest waterfall, other than Niagara Falls, east of the Mississippi River. In the summer of 1778 Hamilton picnicked atop the roaring falls with George Washington and the Marquis de Lafayette. He realized that the roaring waters of the Great Falls could provide an endless source of power for a great industrial city. It was the middle of the American Revolution, but already Hamilton was thinking ahead to the economic future.

In 1792, with the Revolution won and a national economy to launch, Hamilton returned to the Great Falls and built the young nation's first planned industrial city. Paper mills, cotton mills, and breweries all followed, with all of them employing wave after wave of impoverished immigrants. In the late 1800s silk mills replaced the cotton mills and, by 1913, Paterson's 300 silk mills provided 60% of America's silk.

Someone had to weave all that silk, and so the mills pulled in weavers from all over Europe. These weavers could not be peasants just off the land. Silk weaving was a highly skilled profession, and so weavers were lured to Paterson from the older silk cities of Europe. Jewish weavers came from Poland and Russia, Italian weavers came from the Piedmont regions of northern Italy, German weavers came, all of them to work in the ribbon silk mills that made the fine and narrow silk used in men's ties, hat bands, and labels.

Most of these weavers were men, but there were some women broad-silk weavers. Mostly, though, the women worked in the "throwing" plants, preparing the raw silk thread for weaving by winding, doubling, and twisting the silk. This provided enough work so that just over half of the silk workers in the city were women, many just teenage girls, or perhaps even younger.

Then there were the dye houses. There were less than a dozen of these in Paterson, but they were all twice the size of the large Doherty mill, employing up to 2,000 dyers' helpers each. Doing this work took almost no skill at all, and it could be learned in a week. For this reason, southern Italians from Calabria and Abruzzi, not long off the land, filled the dye houses. Working in teams of seven or eight under the supervision of a dyer, the helpers mixed toxic chemicals into the silk yarn in large tubs. The dye houses were filthy and filled with steam and lethal fumes, hot in the winter and unbearable in the summer. Boiling chemicals burned the skin off the hands of the helpers and all of them bore the scars of chemical burns. Often the chemicals sloshed onto the always-slippery floor and, although the helpers wore wooden clogs, nevertheless their feet were usually wet with the acidic chemicals.

For this deadly work the helpers were officially paid $11 a week, but the work was seasonal and they were often unemployed, so it averaged out to about $6 a week annually. They envied the skilled broad-silk and ribbon silk weavers, who averaged up to $14 a week. The weavers, for their part, disdained the dyers' helpers. This was true even of the Italian weavers from the Piedmont. There was very little that urbanized northern Italian weavers and rural southern Italian dyers' helpers had in common. They even spoke different dialects and could hardly understand each other.

The "Americans" made no such distinctions. Both the mill owners and the city authorities treated all Italians, whether northern or southern, with the same contempt they treated the Polish and Russian Jews who worked in their factories. Skilled or unskilled, it made no difference to them. All southern and eastern European immigrants were, to them, a lower breed of humanity. Indeed, they were hardly human at all. They were simply dagoes and wops, kikes and sheenies.

The fact that a large part of these "Americans" were Irish, who had once been thought barely human themselves, was an irony lost on the Americanized Irish. Their forbears had flooded into the country in the 1840s at the height of the Irish Potato Famine. Despised and disdained as alien Catholic trash by Anglo Protestant "natives," the Irish, over the years and the generations, had shed their foreign taint as drunken "paddies" and had worked themselves up to become accepted as "white" and as "American." Two major ladders upward to respectability, or at least to power, were politics and the police. Thus, the mayor of Paterson was now an Irishman, Andrew McBride, and the Chief of Police, John Bimson, was another Irishman. Most of the police force was also Irish.

The fact that the Irish were Catholic, as were the Italians, was unimportant. The Irish and the Italians did not speak the same language, and barely acknowledged that they shared the same religion. Certainly, Italian Catholics did not attend Irish Catholic churches. And, although Italians were the largest ethnic group in Paterson, there was only one church for all of them. As it happened, the church served mostly southern Italians, so there wasn't the conflict with the northern Italians in the church there might otherwise have been. This was because the urbanized Piedmontese were largely secular and anti-clerical. Indeed, it was from these northern Italians that most of Paterson's anarchists came.

Paterson had a long tradition of anarchism. The ideology was widespread in Italy, and the immigrants from "the old country" brought it to Paterson with them. Thus, by the 1890s Paterson had become the center of international Italian anarchism. These anarchists believed in "propaganda of the deed," which basically meant assassination. It was no surprise to anyone, therefore, that in 1900 a Paterson immigrant anarchist returned home to Italy to assassinate King Umberto I.

Dismayed by the perceived dangers of the local Italian anarchists, the Anglo-Irish "Americans" vowed to get rid of them. As part of this effort, they made John Bimson, who had joined the police force in 1877, the Chief of Police in 1906. His mandate was to suppress the Italians.

In 1907 the Anglo-Irish seized political control of the city when they instituted a new "progressive" business-oriented form of government. The elected Board of Aldermen was stripped of power and replaced by an unelected Board of Commissioners, with all the members, mostly manufacturers, appointed by the mayor. It was this unelected Board of Commissioners, well insulated from the increasingly Italian electorate, which controlled the politics of the city, and controlled the police. They increased the size of the police force by 50%; created a mounted police division; bought newly invented motorized police wagons; and opened a police sub-station in the heart of the Italian neighborhood to better keep an eye on the always-troublesome Italians. In 1908 the Board of Commissioners banned the local Italian anarchist newspaper and finally harassed local Italian anarchist organizations out of existence.

But other dissident groups remained. There were no unions in the mills. The United Textile Workers, part of the American Federation of Labor, the AFL, was composed of "American" skilled craft workers and spurned the immigrant mill workers as a polyglot population impossible to organize. That union had no interest in Paterson. But Max Gerstein was typical in belonging to the Workmen's Circle, a Jewish fraternal society steeped in the socialist tradition and strongly pro-union.

Max also belonged to the Socialist Party, as did many other mill workers, especially the broad-silk and ribbon weavers. Louis Magnet, for instance, the leader of the largely native and mostly English-speaking ribbon weavers, was also a Socialist Party member. Indeed, workers in the adjacent town of Haledon had just elected a Socialist Party mayor.

Then there was the Industrial Workers of the World, the IWW. Many of the same weavers who belonged to the Socialist Party also belonged to Paterson's Local Union 152 of the IWW. Unlike the AFL, the IWW was interested in organizing the unorganized immigrant mill workers. In fact, they had won a great and famous victory for the immigrant cotton mill workers of Lawrence, Massachusetts, just the year before. Max knew many of these local Paterson Wobblies, as they were called. There was Edward Zuersher, for example. The son of a ribbon weaver, Zuersher was born in New York City's Yonkers neighborhood. His family moved to Paterson in the 1880s and he began weaving ribbon in a local mill in 1903. He was the Secretary-Treasurer of the IWW's Local Union 152, and also a Socialist Party member.

Max also knew Adolph Lessig, a broad-silk weaver in the David mill and the chief of Local Union 152. Lessig had been weaving cotton and silk since the 1880s. He came to Paterson in 1902 and, in 1905, joined the IWW the same year it was founded.

Ewald Koettgen was another local IWW leader Max knew well. Koettgen, a tall gaunt man with a deeply lined face, had been a Paterson silk worker since the 1880s. He was the only full-time Local Union 152 organizer, for which the IWW paid him $18 a week, the standard pay for their organizers. The year before, 1912, he had won a seat on the IWW's National Board. And, just that month, he had also been elected chairman of the IWW's National Textile Union.

Koettgen devoted himself to his organizing job, and never seemed to rest. Already he had recruited 500 Paterson weavers into IWW Local Union 152. The IWW, then, had deep roots among Paterson's weavers. Indeed, Max Gerstein was one of those weavers Koettgen had recruited. But, like most other Paterson weavers, Max saw no contradiction between belonging to both the IWW and the Socialist Party. As he saw it, the Wobblies were the industrial union side of the struggle and the Socialists were the electoral side. You needed both sides to be successful.

It was natural, therefore, that when the bosses at the Henry Doherty broad-silk mill announced that they were going to double the number of looms the weavers tended, Max and every other weaver in the mill resisted. Now, the owners said, all weavers would have to tend two looms in front of them, and two looms behind them. The weavers called this a "speed up." The mill owners called it "progress," as it would double each worker's productivity. The four-loom standard was being introduced elsewhere in the industry, it was time to introduce it to Paterson, and the big Doherty mill would be the first to do so.

However, while productivity would be doubled, wages would not be doubled. They never were. The workers had already experienced this when they went from tending one loom to tending two. As before, everyone would be working twice as hard, but for the same rate of pay. All profits from the increased productivity would go into the pockets of the bosses. And, if tending four looms meant "progress," why not make every weaver responsible for six looms, and have even more "progress"? Max and every other worker in the Doherty mill, Socialist or not, Wobbly or not, knew what kind of "progress" this was; it was pure and simple exploitation.

In addition, every weaver understood another long-term danger of such a speed-up. With each weaver producing twice as much, fewer weavers would be needed. It would mean filling the streets of Paterson with unemployed weavers, and this, in turn, would lead to a general reduction in wages. If weavers objected to working twice as hard for the very same pay, or perhaps even less pay, they were free to quit. There would be plenty of unemployed and hungry weavers waiting just outside the mill gates, eager to take their places at the four looms. Accepting the new four-loom workload, therefore, was simply unacceptable to the weavers.

So the weavers chose four of their number as a delegation to talk to the plant managers about their concerns. They were meeting with the managers this very morning. No doubt Max and the other weavers would be informed of the progress of the talks sometime today. Max set his thoughts aside and focused on adjusting the silk threads on the two looms in front of him. Two looms are quite enough to deal with, he thought.

A little later an apprentice weaver, a boy in his early teens, came walking down the line. He spoke for a short time to each weaver at his looms, and then walked on. Max thought this might be the news of the meeting he was waiting for. At last the boy reached him. Max nodded and, still carefully watching the flowing silk on his clattering looms, asked, "What's the news?"

"Management refuses to talk about the four looms. All four members of our delegation were fired for being troublemakers."

Anger instantly flared in Max. He couldn't say he was surprised. Firing was a known risk. Anyone who raised a voice in protest to management decisions faced the danger of dismissal. The four members of the delegation had only agreed to do so if everyone else in the mill backed them up. Every weaver, including Max, pledged they would walk out if the delegation members were fired. On those conditions, the delegation went to speak with management.

And, for doing so, they were fired.

Max and every other weaver in the Doherty mill knew what they had to do. He looked out the filthy window near his looms at the pale winter sunlight just beginning to shine through the cracked glass. Then he noticed the threads on his loom begin to wander out of alignment and he knew they would break in an instant if he didn't reach out to straighten them.

Max did not reach out. The threads caught, became entangled, and suddenly snapped. The power looms automatically shut off, and the gliding shuttles shuddered to a stop. Max smiled at the ruined silk. "It's going to take half a day to fix this mess," he thought.

Then he walked over to the weaver nearest him and told him to shut it down. The weaver looked at Max and didn't need to ask why. The weaver stepped back from his looms and watched the silk threads quickly tangle and break. Then the two weavers walked on down the line and spoke to other weavers. Looms began to shut down all over the floor as they became entangled in broken silk. Soon the entire shop was silent.

The weavers opened the doors of the Doherty mill and Max Gerstein led them out into the snow-covered streets of Paterson. As Max walked out of the mill he shivered in the chill winter air. "It's a cold day in Paterson," he thought to himself, "but it's going to be a cold day in Hell before I walk into this mill again."

Big Bill in Bohemia

Big Bill Haywood was not afraid of public speaking. He'd been doing it for years, all over the country. Indeed, he had become the IWW's star jawsmith. His audiences were usually composed of rough-hewn workingmen, men who understood and welcomed his simple blunt language. But the audience before him today was comprised entirely of educated young women, New York school teachers. What could he possibly say to them, and not sound like an uneducated buffoon? Perhaps it was a mistake to come here today, he thought to himself. I doubt any good will come of this. Big Bill shifted his weight uncomfortably in his wooden chair and brushed his hand through his unruly hair, trying unsuccessfully to smooth it down.

Big Bill had been born and raised in Salt Lake City, Utah, a long way from New York City. With his Stetson cowboy hat and western drawl he was as western as tumbleweed. He had begun working in the silver mines of Nevada at age 15. He was a hard-bitten man who knew what hard labor meant.

But now, ever since his release from jail in Boise, Idaho, back in the summer of 1907, Big Bill had been touring the country as a celebrated speaker. It was that stint in jail, accused of ordering the murder of the ex-governor of Idaho, which had made him a radical celebrity, a working class hero, in demand everywhere. It had also given him the aura of a dangerous man out of the half-civilized West, a man capable of violence, a man you did not want to anger.

His physical appearance added to his mystique. He was almost six feet tall and weighed 240 lbs., which was why they called him "Big Bill." He had lost his right eye long ago and his eyelid drooped down over the ruined eye, giving him a sinister look. He turned his head slightly to the right when he looked at you with his good left eye. This gave him the impression of a bull getting ready to attack. It was said he had lost his eye in a knife fight in a Colorado mining town. It was clear to all who saw him that Big Bill was a dangerous man.

In reality, Big Bill had lost the eye as a boy of nine while whittling a slingshot out of a stick. The knife had slipped off the stick and struck him in the eye. Nor was Big Bill actually a dangerous man, except to the bosses. They feared his legend, a legend they helped create by labeling him a dangerous man. By doing so they showed their fear of him, and thus endowed him with power. As fear and power are the fountainheads of faith, this had increased the faith of workers everywhere in Big Bill, the conquering champion of the downtrodden.

Big Bill had been jailed in Idaho in 1906 for conspiracy to assassinate Frank Steunenberg, the former governor of the state. Big Bill was then a leader of the Western Federation of Miners, the WFM, a fighting union that was leading a bloody struggle to organize hardrock miners everywhere in the Rocky Mountain region. The union had led violent strikes at Cripple Creek and Telluride, Colorado, and also, in 1899, at Coeur d'Alene, Idaho. However, as governor, Steunenberg had crushed the WFM local union in Coeur d'Alene with martial law and mass incarceration of striking miners in bullpens.

By 1905 Steunenberg was no longer in office, but bitterness toward him still festered. On December 30th of that year he opened the front yard gate to his home in Caldwell, Idaho, setting off a bomb that killed him. Harry Orchard, a 40-year-old drifter, and the only stranger in the small town, was soon arrested. Bomb making material was found in his hotel room.

It was soon revealed that Harry Orchard had been a miner during the Cripple Creek strike, where the miners had also used bombs in their battle with the bosses. He had also served a short time as the bodyguard of Charles Moyer, the president of the Western Federation of Miners. He claimed he had been ordered to assassinate Steunenberg by Moyer. And, he soon "remembered", the union's secretary-treasurer, Big Bill Haywood, the real power in the union, had also been part of the plot. What is more, but only for lenient consideration by the prosecution, he was willing to turn state's evidence and testify against the two union leaders. The Powers That Be leaped at this opportunity to send the two powerful union men to long prison terms for murder.

Idaho Governor Frank Gooding took charge of the effort to avenge his predecessor. He appointed William Borah, the same man who had tried and convicted the Coeur d'Alene WFM strike leaders in 1899, to prosecute the case. Then he hired James McParlan, head of the Denver Bureau of the Pinkerton Detective Agency, to lead the investigation.

James McParlan was a legendary Pinkerton agent. In 1875, as just another ordinary Irish coal miner, he had infiltrated the "Mollie Maguires" in the coal-mining regions of eastern Pennsylvania. The Mollie Maguires were reputed to be a secret group of Irish coal miners who carried out assassinations and bombings in the Schuylkill County anthracite coalfields. McParlan's testimony against them resulted in mass trials, mass convictions, and mass hangings. As his reward, the lowly Pinkerton agent was promoted to head the Denver office. There he had waged a long war against the Western Federation of Miners. He was the obvious man for this new job, and he was eager to do it.

The governor of Colorado refused to extradite Charles Moyer and Big Bill to Idaho on what he deemed to be the dubious testimony of the confessed assassin. McParlan, therefore, oversaw the extra-legal kidnapping of Moyer and Haywood in Denver by his agents. Both men were secretly hustled off to Idaho and jailed in Boise. Their trials were separated and Big Bill was brought to trial first, with Henry Orchard, the confessed assassin, the sole witness against him.

Not only the Western Federation of Miners, but also the entire labor movement, indeed, the entire radical world, saw the kidnapping and resulting trial as a frame-up and an obvious attempt to destroy the WFM. Clarence Darrow, the famed "attorney for the damned," took charge of the defense. Workers everywhere rallied in support of the two union officials, and Big Bill's trial became a *cause celebre*. Every workingman in America felt himself to be on trial with Big Bill Haywood. Workers marched in cities across America demanding the release of the two men. In Boston, after a three-hour parade of union men marching 50-abreast up Commonwealth Avenue, over 100,000 workers rallied on Boston Common demanding freedom for the two men. For a year and half Big Bill's name was on every worker's lips, as he became the most famous political prisoner in America. In 1906, even while he was still in jail awaiting trial, Big Bill received 16,000 votes for governor of Colorado.

Then, in July, 1907, the jury rendered its verdict: Not Guilty. Big Bill walked out of jail in Boise and into legend. After that, the prosecution didn't even bother to bring union president Charles Moyer to trial, and charges against him were dropped. Chastened by the experience, however, Moyer and the Western Federation of Miners moved toward conservative trade unionism. In April of 1908 the Federation removed the increasingly radical Big Bill from its Executive Board and expelled him.

But the Socialist Party welcomed him. Socialist Party leader Eugene V. Debs called Big Bill the "Lincoln of Labor." He was quickly elected to the National Executive Committee of the Socialist Party, and Debs said that the popular hero should be party's presidential nominee in 1908. Big Bill said he was honored, but declined the honor, which made him even more honored than before.

And everyone wanted to hear the great man speak. No longer a union official, Big Bill turned to the lucrative lecture circuit, sometimes earning up to $1,000 a month as the famous champion of labor. Big Bill had been a teenage usher at a theater in Salt Lake City. As such, had seen Edwin Booth, America's foremost Shakespearean actor, declaim on the stage. Booth's highly theatrical style made a big impression on him. When speaking to an audience of workingmen, therefore, Big Bill emulated Edwin Booth, speaking boldly with powerful gestures. Even if the audience did not speak English, they understood Big Bill.

In 1910 the Socialist Party sent him to Europe as one of its seven delegates to the Copenhagen Congress of the Second International of socialist organizations. There he brushed shoulders with such communist luminaries as the Russian Vladimir Lenin and the German Rosa Luxemburg, and even the Italian anarchist Carlo Tresca. Big Bill was no theorist or intellectual, he was a hard rock miner, and so he sat mute among the famous working class leaders from around Europe, hardly grasping what they were arguing about.

Afterward, however, Big Bill was welcomed before rank and file audiences across Europe. At a mass meeting of striking coal miners in Wales, British Labour Party leader Ramsey McDonald found him to be an impressive speaker. "He is a bundle of primitive instincts," McDonald said, "a master of direct statement. He is a torch before a crowd of workers. He made them see things his way. His appeals moved them to wild applause, and their hearts bounded to be up and doing."

From Wales Big Bill went to France, where he was vastly impressed by the recently successful general strike on the railways, led by the workers' syndicates. Big Bill became an even more fervent believer in syndicalism and the possibilities of the general strike. Such direct action, he thought, was far more effective than incremental political action.

This put him at odds with many in the Socialist Party, however, as it was totally committed to incremental political action. At the same time, it drew him even more strongly into the orbit of the Industrial Workers of the World, which Big Bill had joined in 1905 at its founding. Thus, when he returned from Europe, Big Bill willingly went where the IWW sent him, eager to lend his blunt oratory and organizational skills to any strike. In 1912 this meant going to Lawrence, Massachusetts, where the immigrant cotton textile workers were on strike. The original IWW organizers in Lawrence, Joe Ettor and Arturo Giovannitti, were jailed at the very beginning of the strike. To replace them, the IWW sent in the young, but hard working, Elizabeth Gurley Flynn and, for inspiration, Big Bill Haywood.

What Big Bill found in Lawrence was a vindication of the syndicalist idea of the general strike. Lawrence was a one-industry town, that being cotton textiles. And the entire workforce, comprising over 20,000 workers from 25 different ethnic groups and a dozen trades, was on strike. It was a vicious and bloody strike, where even immigrant children were beaten and pulled from their mothers' arms as the mothers tried to send them out of town for their safety. The Massachusetts governor declared martial law sent in the militia. Harvard students gleefully rushed to Lawrence to join in attacks on the despised immigrant workers. America's class war came graphically to life in Lawrence in 1912.

But, after two months of bloody combat, the bosses crumpled and the IWW and the immigrant workers won. It was a triumphant breakthrough into the East for the Western-based IWW. It emerged from the strike with the aura of invincibility, and as the only hope for the immigrant masses of the Eastern mill towns.

And Big Bill and his legend emerged from the strike bigger than ever, even more dangerous in the eyes of the bosses, and even more their unbeatable champion in the eyes of workers. Big Bill's magnetic presence was in demand everywhere, and he went where he was called. At the mere mention of his name as he strode ponderously on stage, his working class audiences broke into raucous applause, whistling and howling wildly.

The Lawrence strike also had a profound impact on Big Bill. He had seen the power of the general strike in action right here in America. Just as his oratory and his mere physical presence inspired workers, the workers' victory through their solidarity and mass action inspired Big Bill. He had seen the Promised Land, and the way to get there was through the general strike. "I will not vote again," he declared.

Which was just what his enemies in the Socialist Party wanted to hear. There had always been a sizeable portion of the party that was uncomfortable with Big Bill's popularity, and with his emphasis on direct action, as opposed to electoral action. The party was committed to elections as the way to the Promised Land. The IWW did not believe in elections. Now those opposed to the IWW had proof, in Big Bill's own words, that Big Bill did not believe in them, either. In the wake of the IWW victory in Lawrence, those in the Socialist Party who had always distrusted Big Bill's membership in the IWW moved to purge him from the party's National Executive Committee and expel anyone who believed in workplace "sabotage," as the IWW did.

Big Bill was unconcerned. He was now committed entirely to the IWW, and would go where they needed him, willing to speak anywhere in support of the Wobblies and the general strike.

And today that willingness had brought him to Greenwich Village's Liberal Club and this group of young female school teachers eagerly waiting to hear him. Big Bill had been reluctant at first. What could he say about the class struggle to such an audience? But Henrietta Rodman, who invited him, insisted that the struggle of women teachers for respect and employment in the New York City public schools was also part of the class struggle. Perhaps it was, Big Bill decided, and he finally agreed to speak to her group.

Henrietta Rodman was a tall and thin woman suffragist and a general troublemaker in her own right. She lived in Greenwich Village and, like many of the feminist New Women of the Village, wore her hair bobbed short. She also wore some kind of ethnic jewelry, sandals instead of "proper" shoes and, for a dress, a straight shift that resembled an old meal sack. It would have been easy for a casual observer to dismiss her as just another inconsequential Village Bohemian. That casual observer would have been wrong. Rodman was not only a public school teacher; she was the head of the New York City teachers' union, comprised largely of women.

Rodman was currently leading a highly public battle against the Board of Education's requirement that female teachers officially report to the Board any change in their marital status, which male teachers did not have to do. Rodman had recently married, and had publicly announced her marriage, as well as her refusal to officially report her marriage to the Board. The newspapers pounced on her announcement, eager to report the doings of the New Women. Of course, the newspapers also salaciously elaborated on her personal life. *The New York Times* reported that the public school teacher and head of the teachers' union was living in a Greenwich Village free love *ménage a trois*. It was a scandal and a travesty.

The controversy found its way into the Liberal Club, where Rodman was also an active member. The Liberal Club was located just above Polly's Restaurant at 137 Macdougal Street. Everyone in the Village went to Polly's. She was a tall and serene woman who, for some strange reason, had become lovers with the short and wild-haired anarchist Hippolyte Havel after he'd broken up with Emma Goldman. The Washington Square Bookshop, run by Charles and Albert Boni, was next door, at 135 Macdougal Street. The wall between the bookstore and Polly's had been knocked down, allowing the free flow of traffic between the two establishments. There was a free flow, also, between Polly's and the Liberal Club above it.

The Liberal Club was a bastion of progressive reformers. But progressive reformers and the Village Bohemians parted ways when it came to issues of sexuality. The progressive reformers claimed that Rodman, living in her Bohemian *ménage a trois*, was lowering the moral tone of the Club, and demanded that she be expelled. The more radical and culturally adventurous Village Bohemians defended her, and so Rodman remained a member. Many progressive reformers did not, resigning from the Liberal Club *en masse*.

And so Henrietta Rodman had free rein to do as she wished at the Liberal Club. And what she wished to do was to invite the famous labor leader Big Bill Haywood to speak to her fellow teachers about the IWW and the class struggle.

Big Bill had slowly and ponderously climbed the creaking wooden stairs to the second floor rooms of the Liberal Club. As he did so, he noticed Hippie Havel waiting on tables at Polly's. He remembered that Havel was both cook and waiter at Polly's. Havel did not appear to enjoy what he was doing, as he constantly and loudly berated the Bohemians at the tables as he slapped down their food before them. "Eat your slop, you bourgeois pigs," he yelled at them.

At the top of the stairs Big Bill found two large high-ceilinged rooms with bare wooden floors. They were sparsely furnished with a few wooden tables painted in bright yellows and oranges pushed up against the walls, and rows of wooden chairs facing a lectern. Cubist art hung on the walls, reminding Big Bill that a big show of such "modern art" had just opened at the Armory. He planned to go, in order to see what all the fuss was about.

There was also an upright player piano, which was useful when the Village Bohemians held their "Pagan Revels" at the Club. These were wild bacchanalian dances where, it was said, the free spirits, male and female, mixed in uninhibited ways. People were said to dress in togas and other exotic costumes. Sometimes, only the costume juxtaposition was *outré*. At one of the Pagan Revels, the anarchist Emma Goldman, who lived close by, came dressed as a Catholic nun. One newspaper described the Liberal Club as "The most energetically wicked free-loving den in Greenwich Village."

Today, however, there did not seem to be any licentious activity going on at the Liberal Club. The rows of wooden chairs were filled with decorous young women who turned eagerly in Big Bill's direction as he entered. They burst into loud applause, and Big Bill smiled at them and removed his Stetson hat. Henrietta Rodman took his cowboy hat and hung it on a wall hook behind the lectern. Then she motioned for Big Bill to have a seat in one of the wooden chairs placed behind the lectern. He did so as she stepped up to the lectern to introduce the man who needed no introduction.

Big Bill looked out over the crowd of young women with his one good eye. Rodman had told him that her fellow teachers would be a welcoming audience. They taught the verities of the culture to their students at the city's schools during the day, she said. At night, however, many of them returned to their small apartments in Greenwich Village, which they often shared with other women teachers. There they changed into more comfortable clothes and went out to a Village café to smoke a cigarette, flirt with a male *habitué*, and engage in furious debate about how to best defy and undermine the dominant culture's verities. They were eager to hear what Big Bill had to say.

Rodman had been droning on about him, with Big Bill paying no attention, when he heard her say, "And now I give you the hero of Lawrence, Big Bill Haywood." The audience of young women erupted into wild applause, with some actually bouncing up and down in their seats as they clapped. There was an electric energy that permeated the room.

Big Bill rose and strode to the podium. He paused dramatically and let the applause die down. Big Bill had learned to do that from watching Edwin Booth wait patiently for his applause to die down back at the theater in Salt Lake City where Big Bill had ushered as a kid. He let his good eye roam over the audience of women. He noticed one young women right up front with the blackest hair he'd ever seen, framing her pale face like a Renaissance Madonna. He smiled a big open grin at her, and she smiled back. Then he spoke. "I am very pleased that an audience such as this has invited me to speak today. I am used to speaking to rough-handed workingmen in the mills. It is a pleasure to see such a fair audience as yourselves today."

The women giggled and applauded, and Big Bill began to relax. Big Bill liked women, and it seemed these women liked him.

"I know I have a reputation for being a rough and dangerous man," he continued. "And, in fact, I have a gun on my person at this very moment. It's right here in my coat pocket." Big Bill tapped his breast pocket as an excited murmur ran around the audience. "Would you like to see my weapon?"

The women erupted in cheers and shouts of "Yes, Big Bill, please show us!"

Big Bill reached into his coat's breast pocket and pulled out his instantly recognizable red IWW membership card, dramatically waving it aloft. "Here it is," he said, "here's my weapon that makes the ruling class tremble in fear, my membership card in the Industrial Workers of the World!"

The women cheered loudly and laughed in appreciation of the trick that Big Bill had played on their expectations. Perhaps, just perhaps, Big Bill wasn't such a dangerous man, after all.

"I used to be a two-gun man," Big Bill continued. "My other gun was my membership card in the Socialist Party. But just a few days ago, on February 4th, my birthday as a matter of fact, and as a birthday gift to me, the Socialist Party saw fit to remove me from its National Executive Committee. Apparently, because I believe in the IWW, I am no longer welcome in the Socialist Party. But, I can see that I am certainly welcome here among you!"

At that the school teachers again erupted in sustained applause and cries of, "Oh, yes, Big Bill, you're welcome here!"

"And you are all welcome in the IWW," Big Bill responded. "We call ourselves the Industrial Workers of the World. However, what we want is One Big Union of all workers, no matter what kind of work they do, and of both sexes, male and female. We do not discriminate, and we want you!"

"And we want you, Bill!" the women yelled. "We want you!"

Big Bill smiled at the women. He would go on to talk about the class struggle and the general strike, but he had already won them over. He had thought it was a mistake to come here today, that no good would come of it. He was wrong.

Afterward the women crowded around him and he handed out the red IWW membership cards until his batch ran out. The women talked excitedly, feverishly, some reaching out to touch his coat. Big Bill noticed that one who did so was the Madonna with the long black tresses he'd noticed earlier. Unlike the tall and thin Henrietta Rodman, with her plain face, bobbed hair, and sackcloth dress, this one was small and curvy, the way Big Bill liked a woman to be, and dressed in a modest but fashionable dress. Big Bill again noted that she had the whitest skin he had ever seen. Her coal black hair falling down over her shoulders emphasized the porcelain whiteness of her skin. Big Bill thought she was right pretty.

"Do you teach in one of the grade schools?" Big Bill asked her.

"No, I'm a high school English teacher."

"And what is your name?"

"Bea Shostac."

"Bee, as in honeybee?"

"No, Bea as in Beatrice."

"Well, Bea as in Beatrice, you certainly look like a honeybee to me," Big Bill said, smiling. "I'm very pleased to meet you. Perhaps we can get to know each other better."

The black-haired Madonna smiled at that, and Big Bill knew that it had not been a mistake, after all, to come speak to Henrietta Rodman's teachers.

A Long Day's Journey Into Night

Until the anarchist Hippie Havel showed up, drunk and angry as usual, Max Eastman felt the editorial meeting of *The Masses* had been going as well as could be expected. The editorial collective had been at it for hours and Max could see the New York sky darkening through the skylight above his head. Dusk was coming on, and they'd been at it since noon. They had already argued over and voted on the stories, the articles, and the illustrations that would go into the next issue. Captions for the illustrations had actually been the most contentious. The artists, for the most part, didn't want captions at all, or didn't like the ones the group finally decided on. It took hours to settle those issues.

Then they moved on to the poetry. Max knew that would be another long drawn out battle. They had just begun reading the poems aloud and voting on them when Havel ran up the stairs and burst into the room. As soon as he discovered they were voting on poems for the next issue, he exploded. "Bourgeois pigs! Voting on poetry? You can't vote on poetry, you bourgeois pigs! Poetry is from the soul!"

Oh, God, Max thought to himself. Here we go again. It's going to be another long day. Why the hell did I ever get mixed up with *The Masses*? Then he reminded himself that he had done so because he didn't have anything else to do and, at the time, thought it would be fun. He had recently finished his Ph.D. dissertation in philosophy at Columbia University under the direction of John Dewey. He'd gotten a post-doc position lecturing at Columbia, but the administration didn't like the subject of his lectures. He was too radical. He had organized the Men's League for Woman Suffrage and was making a name for himself in local circles as a public speaker on the subject. But, he was also speaking his mind in his classes. The administration felt a controversial subject like votes for women had no place in the curriculum, so there was a parting of the ways. That was fine with Max, as that would give him time to write poetry and essays, which he wanted to do more than teach. But, he'd have to find some way to support himself.

Then he met the radical artist Art Young at a dinner in honor of socialist writer Jack London. He mentioned to Young that he was looking for a part-time job in the service of socialism. The artist replied that he had just the job for him at *The Masses*. Max knew about the magazine. It had been launched in January, 1911, as a radical monthly "devoted to the interests of the working people." It published muckraking articles, as well as stories, poems, and illustrations of the noble proletariat. Of course, it lost money. For a while, though, one of the "Radical Rich" so essential to such publications kept it going. This benefactor was Rufus Weeks, Vice President of the New York Life Insurance Company, who also happened to be a member of the Socialist Party. Rufus Weeks, however, finally decided he'd reached the limit of the discretionary income he was willing to lose on a proletarian magazine and he pulled out.

The writers and artists who worked on the magazine, however, socialists such as "Ash Can" artist John Sloan and Art Young, weren't willing to let the magazine go under. They looked around for someone with connections to helm the magazine, and Art Young told them about Max Eastman. Max came from a financially comfortable background, was tall and incredibly handsome, and oozed charisma. As a poet, he had the artistic talent they wanted, and as sophisticated charmer he could finagle the money from the Radical Rich the penniless project needed. And he was looking for a job.

The editorial collective quickly agreed on Max, and John Sloan sent him a note written with his paintbrush on a ripped-off piece of drawing paper: "You are elected editor of *The Masses*. No pay."

When Max received the note, he was dubious. He wanted to be a writer, not an editor, and he needed a paying job that gave him enough to actually pay his rent and put food on his table. He contacted Art Young and told him he didn't want to be an editor, and certainly didn't want to work for free. Young told him being editor of *The Masses* would be no work at all, as the editorial collective made all the decisions. Also, they would pay him a nominal salary, once the magazine got back on its feet.

Max was still dubious, but agreed to come to an editorial meeting and meet the others involved in the magazine. The meeting was at *The Masses* building, a three-story wooden structure at 91 Greenwich Avenue in the heart of the Village. The first floor was a storefront with a large window and "The Masses Publishing Co." painted on the glass. Beneath this was a row of books and a small sign saying, "Radical Literature." The windows on the floors above had wooden shutters. Some of them were missing slats; others were hanging askew on their hinges. None of this was encouraging. Max opened the double front doors and climbed the stairs to the top floor, where the meeting was held. He entered a room littered ankle-deep with manuscripts scattered everywhere across the wooden floor. An open skylight in the ceiling did nothing to alleviate the haze of cigarette smoke that made him cough.

Art Young spied him and rushed over to grasp his hand. "Max! Welcome to *The Masses*." Then Young introduce him around. One of the people he met was Charles Winter, who Young introduced as the paste-up man. Max asked what that was, and Charles Winter showed him how to paste up a dummy copy of the magazine. He took long strips of galleys and cut them to fit the space on a magazine page. Then he took a brush and coated the back of a galley with glue from a mucilage pot and stuck it on the dummy page. For Max, this was fun. It combined the infantile delight of cutting out paper dolls with the adult satisfaction of thinking you were actually doing something to mold public opinion.

No one else in the group was doing anything at all, except lounging in ratty overstuffed chairs, smoking, drinking beer, and talking. All of the talk was radical talk, but it was not just talk about stuffy socialism, as Max had expected. It was free-thought talk about everything that was happening in the world. There was in their talk, Max felt, a sense of universal revolt and regeneration, of the just-before-dawn of a new day in American art and literature and living-of-life, as well as in politics. Everyone there felt they were on the cusp of a new age, in which everything was going to radically change.

Max quickly felt at home. He never more warmly enjoyed people, and he felt the feeling was mutual. He agreed to work on the next issue, the belated January, 1913 issue, which would carry an appeal for funds to re-launch of the magazine. If the appeal was successful, they would pay him a salary.

For that issue one of the writers in the group, John Reed, wrote a manifesto, which Max polished. Reed was a recent 1910 Harvard grad in his early twenties who had just come down to New York from Cambridge. The big muckraking journalist Lincoln Steffens was a family friend of Reed's and had gotten him a copy-editing job at the *American Magazine*. This paid just enough for him to pay the rent he shared with three

Harvard classmates in a once-respectable brownstone at 42 Washington Square South.

In the meantime, Reed sold enough articles, stories, and poems to other magazines in town that he had acquired a name for himself as an emerging talent. However, Reed couldn't get the commercial magazines to publish the kind of stories he really felt compelled to write, stories about immigrant low-lifes and Lower East Side prostitutes. But, *The Masses* would do that. In this first new issue Reed would have a story, "Where the Heart Is," describing the life of one such streetwalker.

The manifesto that Reed and Max settled on caught the essence of the new version of *The Masses*. "This magazine is owned and published co-operatively by its editors," it said. "It has no dividends to pay, and nobody is trying to make money out of it. A Revolutionary and not a Reform magazine; a magazine with a sense of humor and no respect for the respectable; Frank; Arrogant; Impertinent; searching for the True Causes; a magazine directed against Rigidity and Dogma wherever it is found; printing what is too naked or true for a money-making press; a magazine whose final policy is to do as it pleases and conciliate nobody – not even its readers."

Surprisingly, enough money came in from that first new issue to pay Max $25 a week as editor and $20 a week for Floyd Dell, a writer just in from Iowa via Chicago, as managing editor. Dolly Sloan, a Socialist Party member like her husband, artist John Sloan, would be the business manager, but she wouldn't be paid. Indeed, no one else would be paid a single penny, not the writers for their stories and articles, not the poets for their poems, not the artists for their illustrations. The magazine was a labor of love and it was an honor to be published in *The Masses*, which they all viewed at *their* magazine. Their pay was the freedom to write and draw as they liked, and everyone else, including readers, could go to hell.

In this, *The Masses* reflected the values of Greenwich Village itself, in which it was embedded. There was no division between the personal and the political among Village radicals. Even their love affairs were political, which was what "free love" was all about. Nor was there a division between art and politics. Every artist should be a rebel and every rebel an artist. They felt every work of art should be a stick of dynamite; otherwise, why bother? And both the magazine and the Villagers seemed to be in revolt against everything. When one puzzled oldster asked John Reed what he was rebelling against, Reed replied, "What do you have?"

Sometimes even the free-spirited Max was himself amused by the antics of the Villagers. Max completely believed in everyone doing just as they liked, whatever they liked, as that was the kind of freedom Max wanted for himself. But, sometimes, it just seemed ridiculous to him, especially when it degenerated into factional squabbling. He parodied the whole thing in a vignette he wrote for the magazine. In it a Village New Woman engaged him in conversation, saying, "A Syndicalist, you know, is a Possibilist Anarchist, just as a Socialist is a Possibilist Utopianist, but a Syndicalist is an Impossibilist Socialist. The truth is, a Syndicalist is an Antistatist, whereas a Socialist is a Statist and a Political Actionist, only an Antimilitarist and a Pacifist. I'm a Collectivist Revisionist myself. Now, it's a funny thing, but my brother says he's a Possibilist Sabotagist, but at the same time an Extremist Communist and a Political Actionist. I don't think that's a possible thing, do you?"

"I thought he was a Chiropractor," Max replied.

So, of course, there were plenty of offended readers. *The Masses* was not the magazine it had previously been, what previous readers expected. Its humor was rude and its socialism drew more upon the vague socialism of H. G. Wells than upon the dogmatic dogmas of Karl Marx. Nor were there any illustrations of noble proletarian workers staring heroically into the rising sun. Artist John Sloan drew his "Ash Can Art" for the magazine, pictures of ordinary people doing ordinary things, such as drinking a cup of coffee at a diner's counter. And, while there were many pictures of young working girls in its pages, there were no pictures of conventionally pretty Gibson Girls. This caused one poet critic to complain, "They draw fat women for *The Masses*. How does that help the working classes?"

But the artists didn't care. They drew for themselves, as the writers and poets wrote for themselves, and the readers be damned. And when subscribers cancelled their subscriptions, Max happily published their angry cancelation letters in the magazine.

Such *joie de vivre* could only go so far, however. Yes, the writers, poets, and artists contributed their work for free, but the printer was still a capitalist businessman who had to be paid. The rent still had to be paid. Utilities still had to be paid. Circulation was never above 40,000, mostly in New York City itself. There were some enthusiastic supporters out in the boondocks. Max was especially appreciative of one young woman out in Portland, Oregon, named Louise Bryant, who sold a lot of subscriptions to people she knew. He wished he had more loyal supporters like her. She was also a writer, and had contributed an article to Alexander Berkman's independent anarchist magazine, *The Blast*. Perhaps, Max thought, he could get Bryant to write for *The Masses*.

But, for the most part, subscriptions did not support *The Masses*, nor did the books they sold downstairs in their storefront. Sometimes they staged a "Pagan Revel" at the Liberal Club for the benefit of the magazine, but that paid enough for just one issue, if they were fortunate. Max, as the "editor," had to make up the difference with his charm and suavity among the "Radical Rich." So, Max raised money to keep the magazine afloat from people like Amos Pinchot and the attorney Samuel Untermeyer, whose brother, Louis Untermeyer, was a member of the editorial collective. He even got the newly arrived socialite Mabel Dodge, who seemed to have her hand in everything, to donate to the magazine.

Even so, costs had to be kept within limits, which no one in the editorial collective except Max Eastman seemed to realize. So, printing costs had to be kept down as much as possible, which meant that the magazine could have only so many pages, and that meant not everything that came in could go in.

And so the editorial collective, about 20 men and women, gathered once a month and sat around a big table under the third floor skylight and smoked and argued and voted on articles and art, stories and poems. Someone would read aloud an anonymous poem, since all the poems were submitted anonymously, just as was all the artwork, and the collective would respond. Sometimes it was easy. All the people at the table would groan in unison and someone would shout, "Oh, God, no!" and the poem would be tossed to the floor, and they would go on. But, at other times there would be angry arguments about the merits of a poem. Then it became hard. That had just been the case. Floyd Dell read a poem that began:

> "Yet we are free who live in Washington Square,
> We dare to think as Uptown wouldn't dare,
> Blazing our nights with arguments uproarious;
> What care we for a dull old world censorious
> When each is sure he'll fashion something glorious?
> Blessed art thou, Anarchic Liberty

Who asketh naught but joy of such as we!"

Floyd stopped reading and put down the poem. Max laughed and said, "Hell no!"

John Reed jumped to his feet, eyes blazing at Max. "And what the hell's wrong with that?"

Oh, God, thought Max. It's probably his. "Is this your poem?"

"It sure as hell is, and I want to know why you laughed at it!"

"Because it's meretricious."

"What do you mean?"

"It's pretentious. It's insincere. There's nothing authentic here."

"It's how I feel."

"There has to be more than feeling in a poem."

"The hell, you say! That's what poetry is, feeling!"

"Yes, authentic feeling, expressed in an unpretentious way. This is just self indulgence." Max looked around the table. "Who else besides Reed thinks this poem should go in the next issue?"

No one raised a hand.

"Well, there you have it," said Max, looking calmly at Reed.

Reed slammed his fist down powerfully on the table, making those around him jump. Max remembered that, besides being a cheerleader at Harvard, Reed had also briefly played football. He was a big boy, and now he was angry, like a little boy. This was going to be tricky. Reed could be a stubborn bully when it suited him.

"I don't give a damn what anyone around this table says," Reed thundered. "This poem goes in the next issue or, by God, I'm resigning from this magazine."

Max groaned inwardly. John Reed was a good writer, one of the best they had. He was especially good at journalism and feature articles. His fiction was good enough for the Dime Novels. But his poetry was plodding and, well, meretricious. Still, Reed was bullheaded and Max could see that Reed meant what he said.

"Ok," Max conceded, "the poem goes in." He looked around the table. "Agreed?"

There was a cowed chorus of mumbled assent. Reed's poem went in.

"OK, moving on. Floyd, read the next poem."

Floyd Dell picked up another sheet of paper from the pile in front of him and began to read:

"What cause could be more asinine
Than yours, ye slaves of bloody toil?
Bleed and groan for Guggenheim!
And give your lives for Standard Oil!"

Floyd put the paper down and looked at John Reed at the other end of the table. "Did you also write this doggerel propaganda?"

Reed smiled. "I agree it is doggerel propaganda, and I did not write it. Hippie Havel sent that in. It's by one of his playwright friends, Eugene O'Neill."

"Yeah, I know O'Neill," Floyd said. "It's his drunken drinking buddy down at the Hell Hole."

Max knew the Hell Hole, but seldom went there. It wasn't his kind of tavern. It was a working class Irish bar just west of Washington Square. Crude wooden tables were scattered around the interior and its floors were covered with sawdust to absorb the spittle and spilled beer. It smelled of sour booze and alcoholic woe, as drunken sods cried into their five-cent mugs of beer. When Hippie Havel wasn't causing trouble elsewhere, or waiting on tables at Polly's, he hung out at the Hell Hole as just another drunken sod. That's where he'd met Eugene O'Neill, a would-be poet and playwright. O'Neill's poems, like the one Floyd Dell had just read, were all drivel. Even so, Havel had published some of them in his one-man anarchist magazine, *Revolt!* O'Neill's plays were a little better, Max thought, more authentic. He should stick to those, and maybe write a play about the Hell Hole and its denizens. After all, a writer should write about what he knows.

"So," Max said, "Do we toss it?"

His suggestion met a chorus of approval, with even Reed joining in. Floyd tossed O'Neill's drivel to the floor.

It was then that Hippie Havel bounded into the room. When he learned that the group had just tossed a poem by his barroom buddy, he was outraged. "Bourgeois pigs! You can't vote on poetry! That poem was from the depths of his soul!"

Max broke in on his rampage. "Look, Hippie, you and Emma Goldman and your anarchist collective over at *Mother Earth* meet and make decisions on the material for the next issue of your magazine, do you not?"

"Oh, sure, sure," Hippie replied, "we anarchists make decisions."

"Well, then?" Max said.

"But we don't abide by them!" Hippie yelled, shaking his fists in the air.

Max bowed his head and massaged his temples with both hands. It's going to be a long, long day, he thought. Above him, it was already night beyond the skylight.

Free Speech in Paterson

    Elizabeth Gurley Flynn had finished speaking and the large crowd of Doherty Mill strikers and other silk workers not yet on strike was leaving Turn Hall when Paterson's Chief of Police John Bimson and his deputies belatedly burst into the hall. They recognized Flynn and Carlo Tresca, standing beside her in the midst of a circle of silk workers, as obvious strangers. They shoved their way through the workers and surrounded the strangers. Chief Bimson planted himself before the strangers and demanded, "Who the hell are you and what are you doing in Paterson?"
    Tresca was still uncertain in the English language, so Flynn answered for the both of them. "We're American citizens and we have a right to be in Paterson or anyplace else we choose to be." Many of the immigrant silk workers in the town were not American citizens, and so did not feel they had a right to speak their minds in Paterson, or any place else in America. Such was not the case with Flynn and Tresca.
    "Don't give me any of that guff," Bimson replied. "Give me your names."
    "I'm Elizabeth Gurley Flynn and this is Carlo Tresca. Who are you?"
    "I'm the Police Chief in this town, and I'll ask the questions. What the hell are you doing here?"
    "We're from the Industrial Workers of the World. The silk workers invited us here to speak to them."
    "Well I sure as hell didn't invite you here. We don't need any outside agitators coming here stirring up trouble."
    "It looks like you already have plenty of trouble here in Paterson without any help from agitators like us."
    "And there'll be a lot less trouble once you two are out of town."
    At that point, Patrick Quinlan entered Turn Hall. He was from the Socialist Party and had also been scheduled to speak at that morning's meeting, as many of the silk workers were members of the party. He arrived too late to speak, and was distraught that he had missed his opportunity. He saw Police Chief Bimson and his deputies surrounding Flynn and Tresca and hurried up to them. "What's going on here?" he asked.
    Bimson whirled and glared at him. "And who the hell are you?"
    "My name is Patrick Quinlan, and I am an American citizen."
    "Are you another one of these outside agitators?"
    "I'm from the Socialist Party, and I've been invited to speak to these men."
    "What right have you, an Irishman, to come here and speak to these wops?"
    "That's none of your business."
    Quinlan's answer enraged Bimson. "Everything that happens in Paterson is my business. Arrest him, boys! Take him to the station!" Two of Bimson's deputies grabbed Quinlan by the arms, twirled him around, and hustled him out of the hall. Bimson turned back to face Tresca and Flynn, his big walrus mustache inches from Flynn's face. "Now the two of you have a choice. You can leave Paterson right now, and never return, or you can be arrested, like your friend. What's it going to be?"
    Flynn shoved her face even closer to Bimson's and stared into his eyes. "We are

American citizens, and we have a right to be in Paterson and speak in Paterson. We're not going anywhere."

"Then you're under arrest," Bimson roared. "Grab 'em, boys!" Bimson's deputies seized Tresca and Flynn and began hustling them out of the hall. It wasn't the first time the two had been arrested, nor the first time Flynn had been called an "outside agitator." The first time was two years before in Philadelphia. She had been speaking at a street meeting of protesting laid-off workers of the Baldwin Locomotive Works. Twelve hundred workers, some of them Wobblies, had been suddenly laid off without reason. The Philadelphia IWW local union called her in to help organize the workers into the IWW and fight for their reinstatement. As soon as Flynn stepped up on a box to address the protesting workers gathered outside the plant gates, the police arrested her. She was placed in a cell at the City Hall, a large building capped with an imposing statue of William Penn, Quaker founder of the Pennsylvania colony.

The next morning she was taken before a police magistrate who told her "These people don't want you outside agitators here!" By "these people" he meant, of course, the bosses. He then fined her $10 for disturbing the peace. The IWW local paid her fine, and she continued disturbing the peace in Philadelphia, Lawrence, and many other places. And now she was an "outside agitator" disturbing the peace of Paterson.

Some of the striking broad-silk workers at the Doherty Mill, like those in Philadelphia, were also members of the IWW, and had called for Flynn and Tresca, heroes of the previous year's successful textile strike in Lawrence, to come and advise them on their strike.

The broad-silk weavers of Paterson had also gone out on strike the previous year, but they had been defeated. The main reason for this was that, unlike in Lawrence, they had been unable to turn their strike into a general strike of all of Paterson's silk workers. The large contingent of dyers' helpers, for instance, did not join their strike.

Unlike the broad-silk weavers, the dyers' helpers did not weave silk; therefore the increase in the number of looms a weaver had to tend did not concern them. What did concern them, however, were the long hours they worked. They worked ten hours a day, with five hours on Saturday, as did all Paterson silk workers. However, while weavers were paid by the finished pieces they produced, dyers' helpers were paid by the hour. When the weavers struck the previous year, the dyers' helpers ignored them, as they felt weaving was no business of theirs. Moreover, their bosses gave them a dollar-a-week raise to keep working, and so they did. And so the strike by the broad-silk weavers failed.

"But that pay raise has now been gradually whittled back to the original level," Max Gerstein said to the group of his fellow Doherty Mill weavers meeting at the IWW Local Union 152. "The dyers' helpers are angry about this. This is an opportunity for us to bring them into the strike." With him were several broad-silk weavers who were also members of IWW Local Union 152, among them Adolph Lessig, head of the local, and Ewald Koettgen, the local's only full-time organizer. Lessig didn't work in the Doherty Mill. He was a weaver in the David Mill, but he was taking an active role in trying to expand the Doherty strike to the other mills.

So was Ewald Koettgen. The strike at the Doherty Mill had taken him by surprise, even though he worked hard to keep abreast of everything that happened in the mills. In early January he had been elected chairman of the IWW's National Textile Union, and had reported on organizing efforts in the Paterson mills. He had emphasized the organization of the town's largely female workforce of shirtwaist workers into IWW Local Union 210, and on Elizabeth Gurley Flynn's inspirational speech to those women workers. At the very end of his report, just in passing, he noted that IWW Local Union 152 of the silk weavers was continuing to agitate against the four-loom system.

When the Doherty Mill's broad-silk weavers struck later that month, on January 27th, it took Koettgen, Lessig, and everyone else in Local Union 152 by surprise. But the local, and the many IWW shop committees in the various mills and dye houses, quickly sprang into action, working to turn the Doherty strike into a general strike. They didn't want a repeat of the previous year's defeat. They sounded out weavers in the various mills about joining the strike, and had received a favorable response.

"Yes, this is encouraging," Lessig said to the group, "but we need the dyers' helpers to actually come out this time, and to do that we need to expand the issues of the strike beyond just wages. They don't care about the four-loom system, and at least their wages aren't below what they were last year."

"You're right," Koettgen replied. "And we do that by speaking to the issue that concerns them the most. Like everybody else, they're overworked. We enlarge the strike by demanding not only opposition to the four-loom system, but we also demand the eight-hour day for all silk workers, with no reduction in wages."

Everyone in the meeting nodded. Not only the local IWW, but the entire American labor movement had been agitating for the eight-hour day ever since the struggle for it in the 1880s had made it a major issue. Every worker in the country felt overworked. The labor movement's slogan of "Eight hours for work, eight hours for sleep, and eight hours for what we will" resonated with every worker. Yes, we want bread, the mill girls of Lawrence sang the year before during their strike, but we want roses, too! That was another way of saying, "We want shorter work hours!"

And so it was agreed. The strike was to be not only by weavers against the four-loom system, but also by all silk workers for the eight-hour day, with no reduction in pay. Through its various shop committees in the mills, IWW Local Union 152 then organized an Executive Strike Committee of 15 to 20 trusted and respected silk workers, and a larger Central Strike Committee of 125 silk workers to make final decisions. This Central Strike Committee would be expanded to include more representatives of various mills once they came out in a general strike. The new Central Strike Committee then agreed to call for a general strike to begin on February 25th. It reserved Turn Hall, where the local labor movement held many of its mass meetings, for a meeting on that date to announce the general strike call. It then asked the national IWW to send them some speakers to encourage the strikers and tell them about the techniques the IWW used to win the previous year's strike in Lawrence.

And so the IWW sent in Carlo Tresca and Elizabeth Gurley Flynn, veterans and heroes of Lawrence. The Paterson workers already knew Flynn. She had spoken to smaller groups of them many times, most recently the women shirtwaist workers the previous month when they joined the IWW. Tresca was needed to speak in their own language to the many native Italian speakers among the immigrant workers who couldn't yet speak English.

"But you don't really need us," Flynn told the large gathering of silk workers in Turn Hall when they arrived. "You've already organized yourselves. You have your Central Strike Committee; you have your Executive Strike Committee. Just remember that there is strength in unity. This is your strike. It belongs to all of you. You must all stick together if you hope to win this general strike, regardless of nationality."

She then went on to speak about the One Big Union. The IWW, she said, wanted to organize all workers into One Big Union, both foreign-born and native-born, regardless of skill or lack of it, regardless of color, religion, or sex. She spoke about how all such differences were used by the bosses to keep workers divided and pitted against each other. Nationalities that had been traditional enemies for centuries now needed to march arm-in-arm on the picket lines, because everyone now shared the same identity. Everyone was a worker. For Flynn and other Wobblies like her, the struggle was for more than a union. It was a crusade to form from the polyglot nationalities of the immigrant workers a united *people*.

"So don't let the bosses trick you by racial prejudice," she continued. "They will try to divide you by telling you that the Jews are going back to work. They will try to divide you by telling you that the Italians are going back to work. You must not believe their lies. The only way you can win this strike is with solidarity!"

The assembly of silk workers cheered lustily and clapped, as Flynn further encouraged them to stand together and win the new general strike. "You work together for the boss," Flynn said, raising her clenched fist. "Now stand together and fight for yourselves! Remember, all for one, and one for all!"

With her last words, Elizabeth Gurley Flynn shook her fist in the air as the Poles and Germans and Italians and Russian Jews in the hall cheered wildly. Then the workers streamed out of Turn Hall into the streets of Paterson, heading for the various mills to begin mass picketing in support of the general strike.

And that was when Police Chief Bimson and his posse of deputies burst into Turn Hall. They were too late to stop the meeting, but were just in time to arrest Carlo Tresca and Elizabeth Gurley Flynn for disturbing the peace, as well as Patrick Quinlan for being an Irishman who dared to speak to wops.

As Bimson and his deputies emerged from the hall with their captives, they encountered almost 2,000 workers still milling about the street. The workers had already witnessed Patrick Quinlan being hauled out of Turn Hall by two policemen and hustled down the street. They were clustered in buzzing clumps discussing what that meant, and what they should do about it. When they saw Bimson and his men drag out Tresca and Flynn, all discussion ended and the workers went wild with anger. A platoon of mounted policemen that had been waiting outside the hall surged into the crowd. Their clubs rose and fell like flails as they beat back the clamoring workers. They formed a protective ring around Bimson and his captives. Then the clot of mounted troopers, with Bimson's men and their captives in their midst, began fighting their way through the surging, cursing crowd.

Despite the continuous and frightful clubbing the mounted troopers meted out, the workers continued to impede the police contingent as it forced its way through the streets of Paterson toward the police station. Once there, Bimson and his deputies rushed their captives inside, as more policemen poured out of the station to attack the workers.

At last a tense standoff emerged from the bloody chaos, as the police and workers faced each other, shouting at each other and panting for breath. Adolph Lessig stepped forth from the crowd of workers, shook his fist at the grim police line guarding the station, and yelled, "You can tell Chief Bimson that he has not won! He may think he has stopped the strike by arresting Tresca and Flynn, but he's wrong. This strike isn't over! This strike has just begun!"

The thousands of angry workers around him cheered, and shook their fists at the police facing them. From inside the station Chief Bimson looked out grimly on the shouting crowd of aroused workers. He couldn't arrest them all, he muttered to himself, but, by God, he sure as hell would arrest Adolph Lessig the next chance he got.

Meanwhile, the news of the arrest of Tresca and Flynn spread like an angry raging fire through the mills. Bimson's arrest of Tresca and Flynn had been a big mistake. What had begun as a strike in one mill was now a general strike in all the mills and dye houses of Paterson.

Big Bill Comes to Paterson

Big Bill Haywood was a man of mystique. He was both a hero and a villain, a figure of great hope, and a figure of great fear. He had been so ever since he had been found innocent of the charge of assassinating former Idaho Governor Frank Steunenberg six years before. To ordinary workers, he was a hero of labor who had been framed for Steunenberg's death simply because he was the leader of the Western Federation of Miners, a fighting union the bosses wanted to destroy. But he had escaped the foul machinations of the bosses and walked out of the trial in Idaho a free man. That turned him from a potential martyr into an invincible champion.

To the authorities, however, he was a villain of the darkest hue, who had gotten away with murder. Whether he was a hero or a villain depended, therefore, on where you stood. He was either a working class hero, or a dire threat to all that was virtuous and noble in American society. His leading role in the successful Lawrence textile strike the year before had served to enhance his legend. Big Bill welcomed the mystique that surrounded him, because people did not struggle without hope. He also accepted the fear it inspired as the unavoidable price to be paid for that mystique.

So, when Big Bill finally came to Paterson on March 7th, he was not surprised to see Police Chief Bimson's men waiting for him on the platform. They also saw the big man in the Stetson cowboy hat as soon as he stepped off the train from New York City with his well-worn black leather travelling satchel in his hand. They quickly seized him, bundled him into a waiting jalopy, and drove him straight to police headquarters, where Bimson was impatiently awaiting him.

Chief Bimson had thought that the arrest of Carlo Tresca, Elizabeth Gurley Flynn, and Patrick Quinlan on February 25th would squelch the incipient strike of the mill workers. Without the outside agitators, the few malcontent workers who had invited them to Paterson to stir up trouble would soon go back to work.

Instead, the strike spiraled out of his control. In the wake of the arrests of the three IWW speakers, the entire city's silk workforce had gone out on strike. By the time Big Bill arrived in Paterson, 9,000 broad-silk weavers, 6,000 ribbon weavers, 6,000 dyers' helpers, 2,000 hard-silk workers (mostly unskilled boys and girls), and 900 loaders, warpers, and quillers were out, totaling almost 24,000 workers. Then the 2,000 mill-supply workers, with little to do because the strike hampered their work, decided to officially join the strike and make their own demands. They completed the chain of silk work from the time the silk entered Paterson as raw material to the time it left as a finished product.

In the meantime, Bimson charged Tresca, Flynn, and Quinlan with inciting a riot, and released them to await a future trial date. Quinlan would be the first to be tried, found guilty, and sentenced to seven years in prison for a speech he never gave. Charges against Tresca and Flynn, who had actually spoken in Turn Hall, would eventually be dropped long after the events in Paterson were over. In the meantime, they immediately plunged back into helping to organize the growing strike wave of silk workers.

Everywhere they went, however, the strikers pestered them with the big question,

"Where is Big Bill? When is Big Bill coming? Why isn't he here?" Big Bill was the conquering hero, the man of the hour, the fearless champion of the worker. The strike in Paterson had blossomed into a major strike, and where there was Big Trouble, Big Bill was expected to be there.

And so, at last, Elizabeth Gurley Flynn sent for Big Bill to join them in Paterson. Big Bill answered the call, knowing what to expect. At police headquarters, Bimson's men roughly pulled Big Bill out of the jalopy and hurried him inside. Once in Chief Bimson's office they shoved him into a scarred wooden chair facing Bimson's desk. The wooded chair creaked under Big Bill's 240 lbs. Big Bill removed his Stetson and casually leaned back in the chair, waiting for whatever would happen next.

Police Chief Bimson glared at Big Bill from behind the desk, breathing heavily with stoked up anger. His big walrus mustache puffed outward with each exhalation. "So you're Big Bill Haywood," he finally declared.

"Indeed, I am. And who might you be?"

"I'm Chief of Police John Bimson, and I want to know what the hell you're doing here."

"I'm here at the invitation of Paterson's silk workers to help them win their strike."

Bimson smiled grimly at Big Bill. "Is that so? Well I've got something right here for you to read before you start causing trouble in Paterson." Bimson opened his desk drawer and pulled out a well-thumbed pamphlet. He tossed it on the desk in front of the man lounging in the chair before him. Big Bill turned his head slightly to the right and glanced at the big letters on the title page with his one good left eye. "An Act to Prevent Routs, Riots, and Tumultuous Assemblies," it read. "Perhaps you'd like to take a look at that," Bimson said.

Big Bill grunted and shook his head. "Thank you, but no. In conducting strikes I've become familiar with most of the legal points involved."

Silence grew in the room. Police Chief Bimson was unsure what to do next. Then he said, "I hear you Wobblies believe in 'direct action.' If you cause any violent 'direct action' here in Paterson, you will regret it."

Big Bill smiled at that. "I assure you that in none of my addresses will violence be urged, nor will any be countenanced. By 'direct action' we in the IWW simply mean the withholding of labor. By 'direct action' we mean the strike itself. The Industrial Workers of the World does not advocate violence, nor will I."

Police Chief Bimson was unconvinced. "That may be, but I've heard you always carry a gun on your person. Is that so?"

"That is what people say, but it isn't so. I carry no gun. Would you like to search me?"

"You're damn right I would, and if I find one, you're in big trouble. Stand up."

Slowly, carefully, Big Bill stood up and held open his suit coat so that Bimson's men could search him. They quickly, but thoroughly, patted him down, finding nothing.

Big Bill let his suit coat fall closed again. "So, may I go now? I believe people are awaiting my arrival."

Bimson glared at Big Bill in frustration, then nodded. "You may go. But if you break the law, you'll land right back here in jail pretty damn fast."

Big Bill put his Stetson back on. He slowly adjusted it until he had it just right. Then he said, "I have no intention of breaking the law. I intend simply to exercise my rights as an American citizen to speak my mind freely."

Then he turned and strode through the surrounding clump of policemen back out of the police headquarters. A large crowd of silk workers waited outside. As soon as they saw Big Bill appear at the top of the headquarters stairs their muted grumbling turned into gleeful cheers. Big Bill Haywood had walked free of police clutches once again! They crowded around him, slapping him on the back in congratulations. Then the crowd, with Big Bill in its center, set off for Turn Hall, where even more workers eagerly awaited him.

Turn Hall, the main hall in Paterson where workers held their rallies and big meetings, was jammed with more than 3,000 expectant workers. As soon as Big Bill and his escort entered, the waiting workers burst into thunderous cheers. As the escort made its way slowly and with difficulty through the throng, hands reached out to shake Big Bill's hand, touch him, to brush his coat. Carlo Tresca and Elizabeth Gurley Flynn were awaiting him on the stage at the front of the hall. Big Bill laboriously climbed the steps up to the stage and embraced "Gurley," as he always called her. Tresca shook his hand vigorously, and gestured for him to step to the podium.

Big Bill did so, and the roaring crowd of silk workers became even more full-throated as Big Bill removed his Stetson and waved it triumphantly over his head. The workers whistled and howled and stamped their feet in wild exultation at the sight of their champion, who had once more faced down the police and had won.

Then Big Bill handed his Stetson to Tresca and gestured for the cheering workers to calm down. Slowly, they did so. Silence fell over the crowd as they waited in hushed expectation for Big Bill's words. So did Gurley Flynn. She felt she only really learned how to speak to a crowd of workers the year before, at Lawrence, when she listened to Big Bill speak to them. Wobbly speakers basically all said the same thing. They carried on simple agitation, fanning the flames of discontent among the immigrant workers. They talked about how America was not the Promised Land it was promised to be. What freedom? What prosperity? And they talked about solidarity, how workers all belonged to one big family, working together for the greater good. They talked about internationalism and they talked about Americanism, the first real Americanism the immigrants had ever heard about. They talked about one nation, indivisible, with liberty and justice for all. The immigrants hadn't found it here, but they were fighting to create it. That was what the struggle was all about. They were fighting to make America the land it was supposed to be.

But Big Bill had a way of saying those things that captured the attention of the immigrant workers. They all understood his down-to-earth language, even if their English was poor. He used short words and short sentences; he repeated the same thought in different ways if he felt that his audience didn't understand what he was saying. He never reached for a three-syllable word if a one- or two-syllable word would do. Words are tools, he told Gurley, and not everyone has access to a whole toolbox. The immigrants usually learned English from their children, who finished school after the lower grades, and so, at best, they had a grade school grasp of English. And many immigrant workers began to learn English only during the strike meetings. So you had to keep it simple, and speak plainly and graphically.

And you had to be patient and supportive when the immigrant workers tried to express their own thoughts, fearfully, haltingly, in their broken English, embarrassed by their poor command of the language. Gurley remembered at one meeting when a Hungarian woman striker stood up and hesitantly began to speak in faltering English. The crowd, whose own command of English was only a little better, laughed at her attempt to speak in a language foreign to her. Big Bill shushed the crowd, and told them to let the woman speak, and to be respectful of her bravery. "We must remember that often the hardest worker is not the best speaker," he told them. The crowd fell silent and the woman, encouraged by Big Bill's words, spoke her own words in her poor English. That, too, was a lesson to Gurley.

Big Bill smiled at the assembly and began speaking. "Before coming to Paterson," he said, "I was under the impression that as soon as I stepped off the train, I would be provided with free room and board at the expense of the city."

The assembly laughed at that. "It didn't turn out quite so badly, however. Your friendly Police Chief merely read me the riot act and told me to keep out of trouble." Big Bill paused and smiled even more broadly. "However, I might find that hard to do!" The men before him laughed raucously at his joke.

When the laughter died down, Big Bill continued. "Then Chief Bimson had his men search me for a weapon. They were unable to find one on me. But, you know what?" Big Bill paused theatrically, as he had learned to do as a teenager while watching Edwin Booth act in Shakespeare back in Salt Lake City. The crowd waited expectantly. "I *did* have a weapon on me!" The crowd gasped in excitement. "I always carry one and I carry it right here, in the upper pocket of my vest." Big Bill patted his broad chest. "I am prepared to show you the weapon. Would you like to see it?"

The men before him erupted in wild tumult. Cries of "Show us! Show us, Bill, show us!" filled the hall.

Big Bill thrust his hand inside his suit coat and pulled out his instantly recognizable scarlet IWW membership card, brandishing it aloft over his head. "Here it is!" he cried. "Here is my weapon! My IWW membership card!" The assembly of workers, delighted to be fooled by Big Bill's oratorical trickery, burst into wild cheers and applause.

"But this is also the weapon of the Italian, the Jew, the Pole, it is the weapon of every worker. This is the highest caliber gun in America. It is the symbol of solidarity. It is the great weapon with which the workers of Paterson will lick the bosses and create better conditions for all workers in this city!"

The assembled workers cheered long and loudly as Big Bill continued speaking. He spoke in simple and powerful sentences, hammering home his points like claps of thunder, so that no one could misunderstand him. "Today I am going to speak on the class struggle," he said, "and I am going to make it so plain that even a lawyer can understand it." Again the crowd laughed. "It's as simple as this: If one man has a dollar he didn't work for, some other man worked for a dollar he didn't get."

Big Bill continued on, his oratory inspiring his listeners. But, it was more than his oratory alone that inspired them. His very presence inspired them in a way that a fellow Italian like Carlo Tresca could not. They were immigrants, strangers in a strange land that wanted their labor, but did not want them. But Big Bill Haywood, in his cowboy hat and with his Western drawl, was 100% American. His very presence was proof that they were not fighting alone. It was proof that their struggle was not a struggle between immigrants and Americans, as the bosses and the newspapers and the preachers in their pulpits claimed. It was a struggle of all workers, regardless of origin, against a common enemy, the bosses who exploited them all.

"Sister and brother workers," Big Bill continued. "There are times in every man's life when he feels that words cannot express his feelings. This is the way I feel now when I look into this sea of faces. You are the men and women who clothe the world.

Regardless of where you come from, you are more important than any judge, lawyer, politician, or boss, any man who does not work for an honest living. You all came to America with the expectation of improving your condition. You expected to find a land of the free. But you found that we in America were the same economic slaves as you were in your homelands.

"I come to extend to you the hand of brotherhood, with no thought of nationality. It does not matter if you are a Jew, an Italian, or a Pole. There is no foreigner here in this hall today except the boss. Do not let the bosses divide you by sex, color, creed, or nationality. The working class is one international working class, and if you stand together, regardless of your differences, you cannot be licked. The bosses can lick one Pole or one Jew or one Italian. In fact, the bosses can lick all the Poles, or all the Jews, or all the Italians. But the bosses cannot lick all the nationalities put together, and together we are going to win!"

The crowd erupted into hysterical cheers, stomping and clapping as Big Bill continued. "It doesn't matter where you were born. It doesn't matter what your religion is, Catholic, Protestant, or Jew, or the color of your skin. It doesn't matter if you are a man or a woman. We are all workers! And it doesn't matter what your skill is, or if you have no skill at all, we are all workers! The American Federation of Labor will come in here and organize like this…"

Big Bill held one of his large, powerful hands up for all to see, his fingers spread as far apart as possible. He seized one finger after another with his other hand and said, "They will organize the weaver, they will organize the loom fixer, they will organize the dyers, and they will organize the spinners, each into a separate union. But *this* is how the IWW organizes…" Big Bill clenched his widespread fingers into one big, balled fist and waved it threateningly in the air. "This is how the IWW organizes," he thundered, still waving his fist aloft.

The crowd went wild, waving their fists in the air in emulation of Big Bill. "This is how the IWW organizes," Big Bill repeated, still waving his big fist aloft, "and together we will win!" And then he began chanting, "All for one and one for all!"

And the mass of Italian, Jewish, and Polish workers began chanting along with him. Regardless of ethnicity, they learned the chant from Big Bill Haywood and chanted it along with him, the sound of their three thousand voices shaking the rafters of the hall. For many of them, it was the first English phrase they completely learned and understood. "All for one and one for all! All for one and one for all!"

Big Bill, the man and the legend, had come to Paterson.

The Wretched of the Earth

Shortly after Big Bill came to Paterson, Rabbi Leo Mannheimer, who was sympathetic to the workers, and who hoped to mediate the strike, encountered Big Bill on the street. "Oh, Mr. Haywood," he said, "I'm so glad to meet you. I've been wanting to meet the leader of the strike for some time."

"Then you've made a big mistake," Big Bill replied, "I'm not the leader."

"What?" Rabbi Mannheimer exclaimed, "Then who is?"

"There ain't any 'he'."

"Perhaps I should have said 'they.' Who are they?"

"The strike has no leaders."

"It hasn't? Then who is in charge of it?"

"The strikers. They're in charge of their own strike."

"But, can't I meet some responsible parties somewhere?"

"I suppose you can go talk to the Executive Strike Committee. It meets openly every day at Turn Hall. But I'm not a member of that, and have nothing to do with it. I'm just here at their invitation as a speaker. I don't make the decisions. Go talk to them. They're running the strike."

The fact that the workers themselves ran the strike was hard not only for Rabbi Mannheimer, but also for Sheriff Bimson and the mill owners to grasp. No one, not the bosses, not the newspapers, not the police and the courts, not even those who dealt with them closely, such as Rabbi Mannheimer, thought the huddled immigrant masses of Paterson's factories were able to run their own strike. Self-organization was believed to be beyond their capacity.

Even the leaders of existing labor unions thought immigrant industrial workers were too ignorant for union organization, too unskilled to have any power on the shop floor, too mixed in mutually hostile nationalities for victory to be within their reach. That was why the American Federation of Labor, the AFL, stayed away from them and the factories where they labored. Better to focus on the highly skilled, American born, English speaking workers, AFL leaders thought, who could be more easily organized in their various crafts.

So, in the absence of the AFL, or even the IWW, the Paterson silk workers organized themselves. The Wobblies, for example, did not begin the Paterson strike. The silk workers themselves began the strike, and had already organized it before Big Bill Haywood or Elizabeth Gurley Flynn or Carlo Tresca ever came to Paterson. Every mill had a shop committee that decided what the workers in that mill would do concerning the strike. That shop committee then sent delegates to the Central Strike Committee, which had the final decision-making authority over the strike. Membership in this Committee climbed to around 300 as the strike expanded to include more mills. The shop delegates told the Central Strike Committee what the shop committees decided, and then they took back to their shops the decisions of the Central Strike Committee. Then, to run things on a daily basis, there was an Executive Strike Committee of about 20 trusted senior silk workers.

But none of the Wobbly notables, not Big Bill Haywood, not Carlo Tresca, not Elizabeth Gurley Flynn, not Socialist Patrick Quinlan, were Paterson silk workers. Thus, none of them were members of the Central Strike Committee. They did not have a vote on the Committee, nor did they even have a voice on the Committee. All they could do was advise. The workers on the Committee could then accept or reject that advice.

But this was exactly what the Wobblies wanted. They saw themselves as the facilitators of working class empowerment, not the embodiment of it. Good organizers, they believed, made themselves obsolete. Their job was to help the workers see that they, themselves, had the skill and the knowledge to not only organize their own labor unions, but to also run the industries in which they labored. "The manager's brain," Big Bill often said, "is under the workman's cap." Running the strike was part of that self-organization.

So it was the Paterson silk workers themselves who organized the major strike support activities and organizations. On March 18th, for example, they elected a General Relief Committee through which the families of strikers could get free food staples, such as bread, flour, rice and potatoes. The Relief Committee also organized three soup kitchens for the single men among the strikers. Each mill also had its own relief committee to keep track of the needs of the strikers in its own mill.

That same day the Purity Cooperative Bakery began its free bread distribution. Immigrant Russian Jews established the Cooperative Bakery in 1905 as Paterson's first Jewish bakery. Its 16 bakers donated their labor and the Bakery distributed 30,000 free loaves of bread each week during the strike. The Purity bakers also donated $50 a week out of their own pockets to the strike fund the strikers set up. In addition, sympathetic doctors and dentists gave freely of their services, while the Association of Jewish Landlords voted to not evict silk workers for rent non-payment during the strike.

Rationed staples distributed by the General Relief Committee were free to the strikers, but the food still had to be somehow purchased. Altogether, around $3,000 per week was needed to support strike relief efforts. A third of this came from the local Sons of Italy, which represented nine different Italian groups in Paterson. They voluntarily levied upon themselves an assessment of $1,000 per week to support the strike. Over the course of the strike the Sons of Italy contributed $12,000 to support the strike. But the bulk of strike support funds had to be raised otherwise.

Thus, fundraising became, after picketing and attending meetings, the most common strike activity, and thousands participated in it. Strikers solicited donations from sympathetic local and regional businesses, as well as local and regional labor unions. The strikers, especially the Jews and Italians, also included in their number many talented musicians, and they performed for benefit concerts and dances. Troupes of Italian guitar and mandolin players also toured nearby towns soliciting donations. Strikers even travelled to New York City and paraded up and down Fifth Avenue carrying an American flag and soliciting strike donations.

Next to fundraising, the main activity of the strikers was marching on the picket lines. Marching on the picket lines kept the strike alive by demonstrating that everyone still believed in the strike, and that no one had gone back to work. It was the most visible aspect of the strike, and the strike activity especially targeted by the police. Over the course of the strike, the police arrested 5,000 strikers, jamming the jails with them. For the strikers, being jammed together in the city, and later county, jails became a badge of honor and another way of showing solidarity. The jails rang with their choruses of *The Internationale* and, when they were released, they returned to the picket lines, to be arrested yet again.

The strike committees of the individual mills organized the picket lines. Thus, each mill was picketed by the workers at that mill, insuring that everyone knew who was doing what. The picket line also made sure those desperate few who faltered did not cross the picket line and return to work. Not many did. When outside anarchist kibitzers, like Hippie Havel, criticized the strikers and the Wobblies for not being more violent, Gurley Flynn replied that there was no need for violence. They had solidarity instead. "We shut the mills down tight as a vacuum," she said, with 95% of the workforce out on strike.

And, for those who, nevertheless, did cross a picket line, always with a police escort, there was the shame that everyone knew who they were, and that they had broken ranks with their fellow workers, that they had become that lowest form of humanity, the strikebreaking scab. Their friends and neighbors and fellow workers cried shame upon them as they crossed the picket line and went into the factory, and again when they came out. Their friends and neighbors and fellow workers and gangs of howling children followed them as they plodded home, calling shame down upon them. Then the neighbors and fellow workers and howling children stood outside the scabs' homes reviling them for taking food out of the mouths of the children of their fellow workers.

Thus, there was always something for the strikers to do, as they knew that the life of a strike depended on constant activities. Strikers couldn't just sit idly at home, stewing over their families going hungry, wondering how they would pay their rent, wondering if they should go back to work. Isolation at home bred fear and depression and defeat. Solidarity and victory depended on the strikers being out and about, doing things with each other to support the strike. They had to be working in the soup kitchens, or raising funds in some fashion, or marching on the picket line.

In addition to these activities, there were always meetings to attend. These meetings were central unifying rituals for the strikers. There were the daily shop meetings and the large mass meetings where Big Bill or Carlo Tresca, or Gurley Flynn rallied their spirits and urged them to keep on fighting. There were also additional, smaller, meetings for the children, and meetings just for the women. The success of the strike depended not only on involving the mill workers themselves in constant activity, but also on involving their families in the strike. Hungry children begging for food and angry wives berating their husbands for not providing that food could drive any striker back to work just as much as a policeman's club. The children and the wives, therefore, had to also become active in the strike.

Singing was a big part of all the meetings. The strikers always had brass bands, or singing societies, or quartets singing at their meetings. Or there would be mass singing by everybody. It didn't matter that they spoke different languages from all over Eastern and Southern Europe. "Everyone spoke broken English," one striker recalled, "but it didn't matter. Everyone could sing." So, if they couldn't sing very well, or didn't know the words, that didn't matter. Their voices were lost in the massed chorus. Besides, no matter what the language, everyone knew the words to *The Marseillaise* and *The Internationale*, which they sang at the end of every mass meeting in Turn Hall.

Sometimes they even made up songs about the strike. At the children's meetings one song went like this:
                Leader: Do you like Mr. Boss?
                Children: (Going down the scale) No, no, no!
                Leader: Do you like Miss Flynn?
                Children: (Going up the scale) Yes, yes, yes!

All of these activities buoyed the morale of the strikers, so that day after day, week after week, as the strike dragged on, their spirits remained high and they resisted as a body the various ploys of the bosses to divide and manipulate them. One such attempt by the bosses came on what they called "Flag Day." The authorities believed the IWW was pulling the strings and running the strike. Therefore, they sought to separate their "impressionable" and "gullible" workers from the avowedly revolutionary Wobblies, and also the American-born from foreign-born workers, by appealing to the nascent patriotism of the workers.

Paterson's newspapers were already hammering away incessantly on how "un-American" the Wobblies were. Now, on Flag Day, the authorities presented the workers with the stark choice between Wobbly syndicalism and the American flag. On March 17th, just over three weeks into the strike, Paterson awoke to find that, overnight, every mill and every street had been draped in large American flags. Flanked by two giant American flags, a huge banner stretched across Market Street, Paterson's main street. "We live under this flag," it proclaimed. "We work under this flag. We will defend this flag." At the same time, the morning newspapers announced that the mill owners were prepared to forgive their misled employees and welcome them back to work. The newspapers, the bosses, and the municipal authorities were confident the appeal to the flag would work, and that the poor deluded workers would clamor to return to the mills.

But no one returned to work. The counter-manipulation against the perceived manipulation of the Wobblies failed miserably. The solidarity of the workers remained unbroken. Word of the ploy had gotten around and local Socialists had printed thousands of cards for the strikers to wear in their lapels or on their blouses. The morning of "Flag Day" it seemed that everyone on the streets of Paterson wore one of the cards. It, too, pictured an American flag, along with the words, "We wove the flag. We dyed the flag. We won't scab under the flag."

At a mass meeting of the strikers that morning at Turn Hall, Gurley Flynn told the workers that it was the IWW that truly represented the American ideal. Naming the myriad nationalities of the strikers, she said, "The IWW has done what no other institution in this city has ever done. It has brought together men and women of all nationalities to work together for the common good. The bosses, who seek to divide us and conquer us one by one, do not represent true Americanism. It is the IWW that represents the ideal spirit of America, of one people, regardless of religion or previous nationality, with liberty and justice for all!"

In response, the massed workers in Turn Hall broke into a rolling wave of cheers, which then merged into the song they all knew so well, the song they sang on their picket lines, the song they sang in their jail cells, the song they sang at every meeting. Regardless of nationality, they sang as one: "Arise, ye prisoners of starvation, arise ye wretched of the earth, for justice thunders condemnation, a better world's in birth!"

A week later, on March 24th, the mill owners began taking down their flags and the big banner across Market Street.

The Secret of the Revolution

The Wobblies had a problem. The public saw the Paterson silk strike as an IWW strike but, in fact, it was actually a strike by the Paterson silk workers themselves. The IWW had no control over it at all. If, for example, the silk workers in their various shop committees, and in the Central Strike Committee, decided to call off their strike, or settle the strike mill by mill, then neither Big Bill Haywood, nor Carlo Tresca, nor Elizabeth Gurley Flynn could make them continue it.

And, after they launched their strike, it was the silk workers who asked Big Bill and Tresca and Gurley Flynn to come and speak to them, to advise them, to encourage them. The Wobblies were essentially just cheerleaders for the strike. For the most part, this was completely acceptable to the Wobblies. They thought of themselves as "agitators," just as the authorities called them. They disavowed leadership on principle, and worked hard to encourage leadership emerging from the rank-and-file.

But the rank-and-file workers were mostly unknown and invisible. To the public at large they were both nameless and faceless. Everyone, however, knew Big Bill Haywood and Carlo Tresca and Elizabeth Gurley Flynn. While the workers were anonymous, the Wobblies were infamous celebrities.

In addition, the world saw the mostly immigrant industrial workers as ignorant and easily manipulated, as incapable of self-leadership. Someone with more brains than the workers had to be telling them what to do. That had to be the Wobbly celebrities. So, as far as the authorities and the public at large were concerned, the cheerleaders were the team captains calling the plays.

And this public perception presented the Wobblies with their problem. If the workers won their strike, as in Lawrence, the Wobblies would get the credit for leading them to victory. But also, if the workers were defeated, it was all the fault of the Wobblies for their misjudgment and for making the wrong calls. Both Wobbly victory and Wobbly defeat were illusions, but the public saw the illusions as reality.

Elizabeth Gurley Flynn, in particular, chafed at this situation. She believed in encouraging the emergence of rank-and-file leaders. Sometimes, however, those rank-and-file leaders made decisions that she thought were wrong, such as breaking off a general strike to accept shop-by-shop settlements. In such a situation, the general strike would be seen as a mistaken strategy and a defeat, and the Wobblies would be blamed for it. "There's just too much rank-and-file-ism," she argued to other Wobblies. "If we're going to be blamed for the defeat of a strike, then we should have more control over the strike."

In the meantime, however, she soldiered on like the dedicated cheerleader that she was. Mostly that meant public speaking. Because they believed in encouraging rank-and-file leadership, the Wobblies encouraged the workers themselves to speak at meetings. And individual workers could, indeed, be cajoled into speaking in their faltering English to small groups of their friends and fellow workers in small meetings.

However, they were reluctant to expose their poor grasp of the language to the laughter and ridicule of thousands in large meetings. That was why the professional outside Wobbly speakers were needed. They were not afraid to stand up and speak to thousands. They had done so for years all over the country. But Gurley Flynn and the other Wobbly speakers always denied that this meant they were strike leaders. They thought of themselves as mouthpieces for the dreams and desires of the strikers. "I have no job to lose," Gurley Flynn told them, "so I can say whatever I please about the bosses, so long as I express your sentiments."

Because Italians comprised such a large number of the strikers, Carlo Tresca was especially important as a Wobbly speaker. Although he was not actually a member of the IWW, being too much of an anarchist even for the IWW, he believed in strikes as radicalizing experiences. For that reason, he willingly supported the IWW in strike situations when they called upon him. An Italian immigrant himself, he could speak to the Italians in their own language. But, even the English speakers among the workers liked listening to him. He spoke in such a fiery and animated style that they didn't have to know exactly what he was saying. They got the gist of it, and they enjoyed his energy.

But Big Bill Haywood and Elizabeth Gurley Flynn were the most popular speakers. In one seven day period, Gurley gave over 17 speeches in Paterson. The women and the young girls especially liked to hear Gurley speak in the big mass meetings. She was only 22, but her veteran self-confidence thrilled and inspired them.

As with Tresca, she also believed that part of her job was radicalizing the people she worked with, fanning the flames of their discontent and focusing that discontent on the appropriate targets. She especially tried to do this in the small all-female meetings she led. She pointed out, for instance, that the women could not afford to buy the silk that they themselves, or their husbands, wove. "Would you like to have nice clothes?" Gurley asked the women.

"Oh, yes, yes!" the women agreed.

"Would you like to have nice shoes?"

"Oh, yes, of course!"

"Well, you can't have them! Only your bosses' wives and their daughters get to have nice clothes and nice shoes! Your shoes have holes in the soles, and your dresses are rags, and that's all you'll get."

Then she would ask the women, "Would you like to have soft hands, like the wives and daughters of your bosses?"

"Yes, yes!" the women answered.

"Well, you can't have those, either. Your hands will remain rough and dry, because you must work to make the nice silk dresses for the wives and daughters of your bosses! Your hands will remain rough and dry, so that their hands can be soft and feminine. Doesn't that make you angry?" And, of course, it made the women angry, because they knew it was true.

In addition, Gurley Flynn saw these small meetings with the women as opportunities for education. Inside herself, she felt that the revolution wasn't coming fast enough. Her very first public speech, at the age of 15, had been on the topic, "What Socialism Will Do For Women." But, after years of agitating in working class communities from coast to coast, she had come to believe that it wasn't good enough to wait for a socialist revolution in the sweet bye and bye. Something tangible needed to be done for the suffering women among whom she worked right here and right now.

One of the tangible things, she had come to feel, was talking about the need for family limitation, about how planning for parenthood meant a better life for the women, as well as their children. As she travelled around the country, she had seen how the lives of poor women were narrowed and stunted by the burden of endless child bearing. Indeed, every woman she met knew about this, every woman she met talked about this. That included the women of the Paterson mills. And, since she saw her role as expressing the dreams and desires of those women, that meant talking about "the secret."

At one meeting Gurley invited Carlo Tresca to come to talk to the women about the goals of the strike, what everyone was fighting for. Tresca stood before the women exuding his confident Italian masculinity and explained that they were fighting for the eight-hour day. "Everyone is overworked," Tresca told the women. "We need more time off. We need more time with our families." Then Tresca made a little joke he thought the women would appreciate. "Husbands and wives need more time to spend together," he said, "more time so they can make more *bambinos*, more babies!" Tresca smiled at the women, pleased with his slightly off-color joke.

But the women did not appreciate it. They looked sourly at each other and began to murmur. Gurley quickly jumped up beside Tresca and said, "No, Carlo! That's not what we believe at all. We believe in family limitation. We believe in fewer *bambinos*, well cared for! *That's* what we're fighting for!"

At that the women laughed and burst into applause. Tresca looked at Gurley, puzzled and confused about what had just happened.

But Gurley knew very well what had happened, and why the women were not amused by Tresca's little joke. She knew very well what they really wanted to know more about, and what Tresca could never tell them. They wanted to know "the secret." That was why she asked Margaret Sanger to come from New York and speak about the secret to the Paterson women in the intimacy and privacy of one of their meetings.

Sanger had been a member of the Socialist Party, but she had let her membership lapse. This was because she believed more strongly in what the Wobblies were trying to do, felt it had more real impact, and so she often worked closely with them. She had worked with Big Bill and Gurley Flynn on the Lawrence strike the year before, and was the main organizer of the evacuation of the hungry strikers' children out of Lawrence. Like Gurley, she was Irish, born Margaret Higgins, the daughter of a socialist tombstone carver in Corning, New York. She trained as a nurse and married William Sanger, an architect. After their marriage they moved to New York City, where Margaret became a visiting nurse in working class neighborhoods.

It was there, visiting the immigrant mothers in their teeming Lower East Side slums, that she became intimately familiar with the horrors they endured. Immigrant life on New York's Lower East Side, Margaret Sanger discovered, was appalling. Fear ruled the slums. The men, sullen and brutal, were usually unskilled and usually unemployed, given to crime and drink. If they had poorly paid jobs, they were afraid of losing them, and the women were afraid of falling into even worse conditions. There was no stable home life. The idle men sauntered in and out of the dark and filthy tenement apartments at all hours of the day and night. They beat their wives and they beat their children, of which there were many.

The women kept to themselves, slinking in and out of their tenement homes on their way to market, Sanger thought, "like rats from their holes." Pregnancy was a chronic condition among immigrant women, and the subsequent childbirth was dangerous for them. They usually gave birth at home. This was because of tradition, lack of money for hospital stays, and fear of hospitals. In their experience, people went to hospitals to die. Unfortunately, many immigrant women also died at home in childbirth. Sanger knew one Italian woman who gave birth at home to eight children, with no professional care whatsoever. The last of them she delivered on her filthy kitchen floor, with the aid only of her ten-year-old son. Under the mother's direction, the son then cleaned up the mess on the kitchen floor, wrapped the placenta and bloody rags in paper, and threw them out the kitchen window into the courtyard below. Sometimes the women in such situations just sent their children to a neighbor's while they put their heads into their kitchen ovens and turned on the gas.

The babies born in such conditions might live only a few hours before dying. The women, always pregnant, worked long and hard to find food for five or six or seven children, who were always hungry. The men, disgusted at the weary, pregnant, shapeless bodies of their prematurely old wives, looked with lusting eyes on other women, sometimes even their own young daughters.

In such conditions, Sanger, on her visits to attend to some poor woman's pregnancy or childbirth, discovered that abortions were main topics of conversation among the women. Again and again the women told her of their desperate attempts to terminate their pregnancies. They tried mysterious potions old wives gave them to drink. They rolled down stairs or jumped from as high up as they dared. As a last recourse, they inserted knitting needles or shoe hooks up their vaginas and into the uterus to kill the fetus. Sanger heard hundreds of such stories. The lives of the women she visited on the Lower East Side were lives of either constant pregnancy, or repeated self-induced abortions, frequently resulting in death.

And every time Sanger visited a woman in labor they always asked her the same question: What can I do to keep from getting pregnant again? They talked about the "Yankee tricks" the "American" women did to avoid pregnancy. Or they said that, "It's the rich that know the tricks, while we have all the kids." If the women were Catholics, they asked Sanger what the Protestants did to keep their families down. They said they would pay her more if she would only just tell them "the secret." When Sanger replied that she knew little more about such things than the women, the women laughed at her and suspected she was holding back the information for more money than they could afford.

Gurley asked Sanger to tell the women about a particular incident that happened the previous summer, when Sanger attended a young mother in her twenties on the Lower East Side. Sanger nodded, and slowly began. The Paterson women were quiet and leaned forward expectantly to hear her story.

It was July, Sanger told the women, and the three-room tenement apartment was stifling. The young mother already had three children, ages five, three, and one. The father, as well as the mother, was devoted to the children, and they both did the best they could to provide for them, but they all lived on the edge of starvation. When the mother became pregnant a fourth time, she jammed some kitchen implement up into her uterus to terminate the pregnancy. When her husband returned from work, he found her unconscious on the kitchen floor in a pool of blood, their children wailing around her.

The husband dismissed any thought of a hospital. There was no money for that and, besides, women who went to the hospital in such situations never came back. Instead, they called for Margaret Sanger. Sanger sat at the woman's bedside for three weeks, fighting for the life of the dying patient. The husband hovered fearfully in the background while neighbor women came and went, helping here and there as best they could. The children were sent to stay with relatives.

"July's sultry days and nights melted into an inferno," Sanger said. There was only one toilet for the entire building, and so everything had to be carried down for disposal, while ice, food, and other items had to be carried up three flights of stairs to the dingy furnace of the apartment. For three weeks, day after day, night after night, Sanger sat beside the bed of the woman, sleeping only in brief snatches, waking to cool the fevered brow of her patient, or to spoon a bowl of soup down her throat.

Finally, the young mother rallied and began to recover. Sympathetic neighbor women came with soups and drinks to congratulate her. But the young mother's spirits did not seem to recover with her health. She smiled sadly at the neighbor women and remained quiet in the midst of all the hustle and bustle. She seemed to Sanger to be despondent.

As Sanger neared the end of her vigil and prepared to leave, the young woman grabbed her hand and said, in a trembling voice, "Another baby will finish me, I suppose."

"We will ask the doctor when he comes," Sanger replied, as they had called for a visiting doctor for a final evaluation. When he came, Sanger told him the woman was worried about having another baby.

The doctor stood by the woman's bedside, looked down at her, and said, "And well she should be. Any more such capers, young woman, and there will be no need to call me."

"Yes, I know," the woman replied. "But what can I do to prevent getting that way again?"

"Ah, ha!" the doctor laughed. "So you want to have your cake and eat it too, eh? Well, it can't be done." He then picked up his little black bag and prepared to leave. At the door he turned back to the woman and said, "I'll tell you the only sure thing to do. Tell your husband to sleep on the roof!" And, with those words, he left.

The young woman began to suddenly weep, as Sanger looked on in horror. The woman grabbed Sanger's hand in a fierce grip and looked into her eyes with a desperate pleading. "He can't understand, can he? He's a man, after all. But you understand, don't you?"

The woman released Sanger's hand and clasped her own together as if in prayer and beseeched Sanger, "You're a woman, and you'll tell me the secret, won't you? Please tell me the secret. I promise, I'll never tell it to another soul, if you'll just tell me the secret. Please, oh, please! It means my very life!"

Sanger felt like she was being tortured on a rack for a crime she had not committed, for she really did not know what "the secret" was. She began to weep herself, and turned away from the imploring woman. Then she turned back to the woman and soothed her as best she could. She promised the weeping woman she would return in a few days and tell her the secret.

But, she did not. She couldn't bear to return to the young woman and tell her that she really did not know the secret. The days passed, and then the weeks, and then the months. Three months later, as she was preparing for bed in her Uptown apartment, the phone rang. It was the husband of the young woman, begging Sanger to come immediately to help his wife, who was sick again. Sanger knew it was useless to go, but she went.

She arrived to find the young mother unconscious. The husband was pacing back and forth, clenching his head and crying, "My God! My God! My God!" The woman died ten minutes after Sanger walked into the apartment. Sanger asked the husband what happened. It was the same old story that Sanger had heard a thousand times before: Death from abortion. The woman had become pregnant once more, had tried home remedies, and then had gone to a five-dollar back-alley abortionist. Death followed.

"It was then that the Revolution came," Sanger told the women listening to her, "but not as it has been pictured, nor as history relates that revolutions have come. It came in my own life. It came after I closed the eyes and covered with a sheet the face of that helpless young mother who had pleaded with me to tell her a secret I did not know.

"After I left that desolate apartment I walked and walked and walked. For hours and hours I walked, my bag in hand, thinking, regretting, fearful of my conscience, dreading to face my own accusing soul. I arrived back home at three in the morning. I entered my home quietly, not wanting to wake my husband or my own three beloved children. I stood at my window and looked down upon the dimly lit, sleeping city. As I did so, the miseries and problems of that sleeping city rose before me in a clear vision like a panorama: The dark and crowded tenement apartments; too many children; babies dying in infancy; mothers sick most of their short lives; women made into drudges; children working in cellars; children ages six and seven pushed into the labor market to help earn a living; another baby on the way; still another; yet another; a baby born dead, bringing great relief; an older child dies, bringing sorrow, but nevertheless, relief; a young mother's death; children scattered into institutions; the father, desperate, drunken, slinking away to become an outcast in a society that has trapped him. Poverty, misery, slums, child labor, ignorance, destitution!

"For hours I stood motionless and tense at the window as these pictures unreeled before me. I watched the lights go out in the city as the darkness gave way to the first glimmer of dawn and a colorful sky shined with the first shimmer of dawn. And I realized that a new day had come for me, and a new world, as well. It was like an illumination. I could see clearly how the big problems of our world all seemed to revolve around uncontrolled breeding.

"I kicked my nursing bag across the room and I ripped off my nurse's uniform and threw it into a corner. I renounced nursing forever. I would never again go back to nurse women's ailing bodies, while their miseries were as vast as the stars. I realized that my work as a nurse was entirely futile and useless in relieving the misery I saw all around me. I was finished with superficial cures, with doctors and nurses and social workers, all of whom came face to face with the overwhelming truth of women's needs, and yet turned away from the truth and did nothing.

"Women have every right to know about their own bodies, I said to myself. I would strike out. I would scream from the rooftops. I would tell the world what was going on in the lives of these poor women. I resolved that women should have the knowledge of contraception. I *would* be heard. No matter what it cost, *I would be heard*.

"Then I set out to discover everything I could about family limitation. I read books in the New York Public Library. I asked doctors. I asked everyone. I spent my time in the hope that I would find the 'secret' women were asking for. But I couldn't find out anything. And nobody wanted to talk about it. I consulted the 'up and doing' progressive women who call themselves Feminists. Most of them were shocked at the mention of abortion. Others were scarcely able to keep from laughing at the idea of making a public campaign around the idea of too many children. 'It can't be done,' they said. 'You can't do a thing until we women get the vote.'

"I had previously cast my lot with the women of the Socialist movement. I listened intently to all the debates, arguments, and theories of this great school of thought. But I could never share their great faith in legislation. Their answer to the misery of women and the ignorance of contraceptive knowledge was like that of the Feminists:

Wait until we get the vote and we come into power!

"Wherever I turned, from everyone I approached, I met the same answer: Wait! Wait! Wait until women get the vote! Wait until the Socialists are in power! Wait for the general strike! Wait for the Social Revolution! Wait for the Great Working Class Revolution! Then everything will be solved!

"But women have been waiting for centuries, and we can't wait any longer. We can't wait for the vote; we can't wait for the general strike; we can't wait for socialism; we can't wait for the Revolution! Women and babies are dying every day, and I won't wait! I *will* find out the secret, and then, I promise you, I will tell all of you the secret!"

Margaret Sanger stopped speaking. All before her the Paterson women were rocking back and forth, weeping and wailing. Elizabeth Gurley Flynn next to her was weeping. They were all weeping because Margaret Sanger had spoken about the secret, the great secret that every woman wanted to know. And once they all knew the secret, then the Revolution would come.

The Blood of the Martyr

Valentino Modestino was standing on the front porch of his home across the street from the Weidmann Silk Dyeing Company when one of the "special policemen" hired by the company shot and killed him.

The special policemen were private detectives from the O'Brien Detective Agency of Newark. The Paterson police focused on the mass picket lines around the plants, breaking them up, dispersing the marchers, arresting those who refused to disperse. Meanwhile, the mill owners hired O'Brien detectives at $5 per day, per man, to guard their homes, their mills, and to escort scabs into and out of the mills. They were a private army belonging to the mill owners, but deputized as "special policemen" by Police Chief Bimson and the police board to act with full authority of the law. They were even more brutal than the regular police, and consequently even more hated by the workers.

On the evening of April 17th, a squad of O'Brien detectives was escorting a handful of scab dyers' helpers out of the Weidmann mill at the end of their shift. Spring sunlight still brightened the day, as it was around 6:30 P.M. Striking dyers' helpers were waiting for the scabs as the detectives came out of the mill with the scabs in their midst. The crowd of strikers surrounded the clump of detectives and scabs. As the squad advanced, the crowd parted and let them pass, only to immediately flow together behind them and follow after them, booing and calling out "Scab! Scab!"

The scabs and their protective escort reached the trolley line outside the mill. The detectives fanned out to guard the door of the trolley as the scabs climbed aboard. The trolley, though, did not move. Strikers massed in front of it, preventing it from doing so. "Scab! Scab!" they yelled at the scabs in the trolley.

For Valentino Modestino, who lived just across the street from the entrance to the Weidmann mill, it was a familiar sight. He had seen it every day for the last two months, ever since the strike began. Even so, he came out of his home to watch the confrontation. Any time scabs entered or left the mill there was the possibility of violence, despite the presence of the detectives. Or perhaps the possibility of violence was there because the detectives were there.

Frustrated with the strikers, who refused to let the trolley move, one of the detectives pulled out his gun and fired a random volley of shots over their heads in an attempt to frighten and disperse them. The circle of strikers fell back in fear. Valentino Modestino fell dead on his porch, hit in the chest by one of the bullets. He had not been involved in the confrontation with the scabs and the detectives, but he was the first striker to be killed in Paterson. He would not be the last.

Everyone knew Modestino had not been involved in the fracas. And everyone knew who fired the shot that killed Modestino. Despite this, the detective who killed him was never indicted for anything. He walked free, and was soon back on the battle lines, escorting scabs into and out of the Weidmann mill. The life of an Italian mill worker, it seemed, did not matter.

Appalled that the detective was not charged with any crime, Adolph Lessig, a local IWW silk worker who was one of the strike leaders, dared to ask at a later public meeting, "What power is there in this town that is greater than the power of the law?" He was sentenced to six months in prison for "inciting a riot."

The answer to Lessig's question, of course, was the power of the bosses. They owned the law in Paterson. In addition to their private army of O'Brien detectives, they controlled the police that constantly harassed and attacked the picket lines. The elected municipal officials, hostile to the workers in any case, had no authority over Chief Bimson and his police. An autonomous police board had that authority. That police board, in turn, was comprised entirely of members hostile to the workers. Indeed, a prominent silk manufacturer sat as a member of the board. Silk manufacturers routinely used their power over the police to name particularly militant workers on the picket lines outside their mills, especially "picket captains," for the police to arrest.

They also controlled the courts. In New Jersey, local elected officials appointed all judges, and in Paterson the elected officials were open allies of the mill bosses. Paterson was located in Passaic County, and the hostile Sheriff of Passaic County appointed the county grand juries that indicted the pickets and the IWW speakers, while refusing to indict any policeman or detective. Thus, for instance, while the detective who killed Modestino walked free, Adolph Lessig was sentenced to six months in prison for asking his question and Socialist Party speaker Patrick Quinlan was sentenced to seven years in prison for a speech he never gave.

Even so, the bosses and the police dared not forbid or attack the massive funeral for Valentino Modestino. Thousands of silk workers crowded into the sole Italian Catholic church on East 19th Street for his funeral service, resulting in standing room only inside the church. Many thousands more waited patiently outside for the service to end.

As pallbearers brought out Modestino's casket, the waiting thousands fell in behind the cortege. The procession then wound its silent way through Paterson, filling the streets from side to side, a seemingly endless flow of mourners. At the Laurel Grove Cemetery, Big Bill Haywood, Carlo Tresca, and Elizabeth Gurley Flynn waited beside an open grave.

The procession halted and positioned Modestino's casket over the grave. The crowd of mourners grew silent, and waited in expectation for Carlo Tresca to speak. His strong voice, speaking entirely in Italian, carried out over the crowd. "Valentino Modestino was the first to die in the struggle. He will not be the last. But, while the bosses can kill a man, they cannot kill what he fought for. Today we mourn fellow worker Valentino Modestino. Tomorrow, the workers will win!"

Next Elizabeth Gurley Flynn spoke in English, mourning a fellow worker and, like Tresca, encouraging her listeners to keep on fighting. And then Big Bill Haywood spoke. "Valentino Modestino was just an ordinary working man," Big Bill said. He held out his hands before him, palms up, over the open grave. "He had the hands of an ordinary working man. But look at the hands of ordinary working men like Valentino Modestino. Look at your own hands. They are hard and scarred and calloused from trying to make a dream come true. That dream is of a better life for all who labor and are weary. And it is for that dream that fellow worker Valentino Modestino walked the picket lines, and for which he died. We will not forget him, and we will not forget his dream, which is also our dream." All who heard his words wept.

Then Valentino Modestino was lowered into his grave. The thousands of Paterson workers who had followed him to his grave then passed by his open grave in a long slow line. As each passed, the mourner dropped a red carnation onto Modestino's casket below. Before long, the open grave was entirely filled with the red flowers. In the bright sunshine it looked like a scarlet pool of blood.

The AFL Appeals to the Workers

On April 21st, the day after Valentino Modestino's funeral, the bosses swallowed their distaste for a union of any kind and brought in the American Federation of Labor to break the strike. The AFL came in the person of John Golden, President of the AFL's United Textile Workers, the UTW. Golden was also a member of the Militia of Christ, a reactionary Catholic organization created to combat radical unionism. Golden also had a long history of special hatred for the IWW. In 1907 he had attempted to break an IWW strike in Skowhegan, Maine. He had also fought against the successful IWW textile strike in Lawrence the previous year. In testimony before Congress he blamed the women and children of Lawrence for the brutal police beating they received at the railroad station when the strikers' children were being evacuated from the city. His UTW also signed an agreement for a small number of Lawrence textile workers and sent them back to work while everyone else was still on strike.

So Big Bill warned Paterson's workers against Golden. "You have had many pitfalls to contend with, and you have escaped them," he said. "There were the police, there were the newspapers, there was the pulpit, there were the special detectives. But now you have the worst pitfall of all – John Golden. He is worse than the detectives. He talks to workingmen in the daytime, but dines at fine banquets with the capitalist class at night. He is the strike breaker."

In early April, with the encouragement of the bosses, Golden opened, for the first time, a UTW recruiting office in Paterson for the weavers and dyers' helpers, offering to waive the usual initiation fee. However, workers remembered how Golden and the UTW had worked with the bosses to introduce the four-loom system in nearby Hazelton, Pennsylvania, and other textile centers, saying that it was "inevitable" and that resistance was futile. Although Paterson's newspapers reported that there was a stampede of recruits to the reasonable and responsible AFL, in fact Golden signed up very few recruits.

It didn't help that Golden, like the AFL as a whole, was disdainful of immigrant workers. "We've tried to organize the foreign textile workers several times," he once explained, "but it's an impossibility. They have radical ideas. They want an organization that will give them instant action. They seem to think strikes are the only things that benefit them, and want an organization that will strike right away. The Italians won't stay with any union that won't strike, and it's useless trying to organize the Jews, because they all talk at once." Thus, when Golden appeared in Paterson, there were no UTW members at all among the striking weavers and dyers' helpers.

Having been unable to attract these workers to his recruiting office, Golden and the bosses called for a mass meeting of all workers on April 21st at the 5th Regiment Armory of the New Jersey National Guard. The bosses had arranged with the state government to make this largest hall in Paterson available in order to accommodate the largest number of workers. The meeting was heavily advertised in the newspapers as a chance for everyone to discuss the UTW's proposals for settling the strike. "It now remains to be seen," declared the Paterson *Evening News*, "whether the claim that has so often been made, that the majority of the silk workers are held out by coercion and fear, is correct."

When the doors of the Armory opened at 7:30 that night, 10,000 workers rushed into the hall, jamming it with a standing-room-only crowd. Thousands more, unable to enter, milled around in the street outside. The enormous noisy crowd inside the Armory immediately began cheering for the IWW and its leaders, Big Bill Haywood, Elizabeth Gurley Flynn, and Carlo Tresca. One worker held up his red IWW membership card and called for the other workers to show theirs also. A forest of hands rose into the air, each holding up a red IWW membership card. The resulting cheers for the IWW shook the rafters of the building and floated outside, where the thousands of workers waiting in the street also began cheering for the IWW.

An hour later, at 8:30, the raucous rally for the IWW was still going on, despite numerous attempts by Golden and other UTW leaders to quiet the workers. Nothing they tried silenced the workers. Finally, the meeting's chairman, representing Paterson's AFL-affiliated Central Labor Council, asked Ewald Koettgen, a local silk worker and the organizer for the IWW's Local Union 152, to come to the stage and ask for silence.

Koettgen climbed to the stage and raised his hands for silence. Eventually the ceaseless cheering for the IWW faded and the crowd grew silent, waiting to hear what Koettgen had to say. As the cheering ceased, Koettgen told the crowd, "We asked the organizers of this meeting to allow a debate tonight between John Golden of the United Textile Workers and Big Bill Haywood of the IWW. We wanted each side to present its views as to how the strike could be settled. John Golden and the UTW leaders told us our request was not acceptable; that this meeting had a set agenda, and a debate with the IWW was not part of that agenda."

A hurricane of boos and jeers erupted from the crowd. Koettgen raised his voice in order to be heard over the noise. "That being the case," he shouted, "this meeting is useless, and I think we should all now just go home."

With that, Koettgen stepped down from the stage and began to walk through the crowd toward the main door. The crowd made way for him and, as he finally departed, perhaps half the crowd of 10,000 workers followed him out of the hall. As soon as they left, however, thousands of the workers waiting on the street outside rushed in to take their places. The hall was soon just as jammed as before. However, the new arrivals also joined in the unceasing boos and jeers for Golden and the other UTW leaders still on stage, and so the meeting still could not begin.

In an attempt to overawe the mostly immigrant workers and cow them into patriotic silence, Sarah Conboy, one of the United Textile Workers officials on the stage, grabbed the pole of one of the two giant American flags that stood on either side of the stage. She then marched back and forth across the stage waving the American flag in front of the workers in an attempt to quell them into silence. Instead of falling into awed silence, however, the assembled workers broke into round after round of cheers for the flag.

And then gradually, as a few began, and then others, and then others, the crowd began to sing *The Internationale*: "Arise, ye prisoners of starvation, arise ye wretched of the Earth, for justice thunders condemnation…" Their voices mingled and the workers sang as one, the sound of their singing rising and shaking the building, "…a better world's in birth!"

At that, John Golden gave up. Police Chief John Bimson and his entire police force had been waiting at the rear of the building. Now Golden called for them to come in and clear the Armory. The police entered with their clubs swinging. They plunged into the front of the crowd, their arms rising and falling upon the workers like harvesters threshing wheat. Pandemonium erupted and terrified screams replaced *The Internationale*. Women, as well as men, fell before the bloody police onslaught, and workers at the rear of the hall rushed for the doors. Anguished screams filled the air as people fell and were trampled in the wild stampede. The police line continued to advance into the crowd, slowly, methodically, clubbing workers to the Armory floor. By 9:15 the police had driven all the workers out of the hall, and then they stood in massed lines outside the Armory doors, ensuring that no one could re-enter.

Inside the Armory, John Golden and the other AFL union officials stood on the stage, looking out over the empty hall. Sarah Conboy still clutched the American flag in her arms. The only sounds that broke the silence were the cries and moans of the bleeding workers beaten to the ground.

Mabel's Big Idea

It began for Mabel Dodge with a dinner party at her Fifth Avenue apartment. It was a small affair with a few friends and new acquaintances. She felt much more comfortable at such dinners than at her grand salons. At the salons, she felt out of her element, not knowing what to say among the celebrated literati. In an intimate setting, however, in her own dining room, at her own large oak table, covered with an embroidered damask tablecloth, she felt at ease. There she could remove her cold and remote mask. There she was able to laugh and talk freely, even grandly.

It was a late April evening. The pale spring evening twilight from the street mingled with the light of the candles on the table. A fire burned in the white marble fireplace in the large adjacent room where Mabel held her salons. A scratchy Mozart sonata was playing softly on the Gramophone. When the record reached the end, Vittorio, her elegantly attired Italian butler, discreetly replaced the stylus at the beginning. No one noticed the brief interruption.

Mabel's Irish cook, Mary Malone, had prepared a repast worthy of Mabel's largesse. After the dinner, Vittorio cleared the table and Mabel sated guests sat back to talk more leisurely. Vittorio poured ruby red wine into their long-stemmed glasses and passed around Curtis cigarettes to the guests, the women as well as the men. Two of the guests were Mabel's good friends Hutchins Hapgood and his wife, Neith Boyce. Mabel and Neith readily lit up. Seeing this, the other women followed suit.

Two of the other guests were John Collier, a long-time friend of Mabel's, and his wife. Collier had brought with him Percy MacKaye, a friend of his own that Mabel had expressed an interest in meeting, as well as his wife. Mabel always wanted to know the well known, and MacKaye was well known as the father of the pageant movement that was gaining popularity across the country. Indeed, MacKaye and Collier had just founded the American Pageant Association to publicize the movement. Collier drew out of his coat breast pocket the Association's first bulletin, just published, and passed it around for all to see. "It lists more than 50 pageants performed all across the country last year," he said proudly.

"What is the usual subject of these pageants?" Mabel asked.

"Historical," MacKaye answered. "Patriotic pageants, enacting in dramatic form the great and noble history of our country. Most of them are of a local nature, portraying the hardy pioneers moving West and settling this great country, including settling the towns that are the settings for many of the pageants."

"I've also heard of a pageant based on *Ramona*, which has become very popular in California," Mabel said. "A pageant portraying Indian life sounds so intriguing." *Ramona* was an 1884 romantic bestseller by Helen Hunt Jackson. It was about a beautiful half-Indian, half-Scottish orphan girl raised by a brutal Mexican *ranchera* in Old California, before the Mexican War. The girl fell into a forbidden love affair with Alessandro, a heroic Mission Indian. The pair eloped and endured many harsh adventures as the novel portrayed the sad story of the Indians and Mexicans whose rights were stripped and whose lands were stolen by invading American pioneers who flooded into

California after the war.

MacKaye harrumphed at the mention of *Ramona*. "Yes, that novel has also been produced as a pageant. It seems to be very popular in San Diego. However, as we survey them, that is not the usual subject matter of a historical pageant."

"I suppose anything could be turned into a pageant," Mabel replied, seemingly oblivious to MacKaye's discomfort. "Not long ago I attempted to turn all of Florence into a *cinquecento* pageant. It was a grand idea. I planned to take over the entire town for three days and recreate the Renaissance in everything: dress, food, work. There was to be no audience, only the actors, who would be the townspeople themselves. We would, briefly, revive the old costumes, the old customs, bring in artisans from all over the world so that it might be a revival of art and beauty, and make everyone ashamed of the ugliness of modern industrial civilization. Alas, the people of Florence were not enthralled by the idea, and my plans fell through."

"That is indeed a great pity," John Collier said. "That would have been the greatest historical pageant the world had ever seen."

"Ah, well," Mabel replied. "Perhaps someday we shall see a great historical pageant like that."

The discussion moved on, until Hutchins Hapgood brought up the IWW strike of silk workers in Paterson. Hutch had written about the strike and its leader, Big Bill Haywood, a few days earlier in *The Globe* newspaper. "One feels that Big Bill Haywood, right or wrong, is a strong, simple man with a unified personality," Hutch said. "His thoughts and his actions go together. You know where he is; you can depend upon him. He led the IWW to victory in Lawrence last year, and he could well lead the IWW to another big victory in Paterson. The IWW, under Haywood's leadership, is becoming a force to be reckoned with."

Hutch's comments caught Mabel's attention. As with Percy MacKaye, it seemed that Big Bill Haywood was another important person worth knowing. "Do you know Mr. Haywood?" she asked.

"Yes, of course," Hutch answered. Hutchins Hapgood seemed to know everyone worth knowing, especially in labor and progressive circles.

"Well, I would certainly appreciate it if you would introduce us one day."

"Actually, I could do that tonight, if you wished. Big Bill is back in town and there's a party for him Neith and I plan to attend later. It's nearby in Greenwich Village. We could take you along with us."

A thrill ran through Mabel at the thought of meeting the dangerous bomb-throwing anarchist. Mabel seldom went anywhere, particularly at night, preferring that people came to her. But she couldn't miss this opportunity. "Why, yes, I think I would like that." She turned to her other guests. "Would any of you like to come along?"

MacKaye and Collier and their wives quickly demurred. "No, I think not," MacKaye said, sounding a little distraught at the idea. "My wife and I must be getting home, it's getting late. However, it's been a most enjoyable evening, and you've been a most gracious hostess."

Mabel escorted her guests to her door and wished them a pleasant goodnight. "I'm so pleased to meet you, Mr. MacKaye. Your discussion of the pageant movement was most intriguing."

"Thank you, Mrs. Dodge. It is most unfortunate your idea for the Florence *cinquecento* pageant didn't work out. Perhaps one day it will."

"Yes, perhaps one day it will."

After her guests departed, Mabel asked if she should have Alberto, her chauffeur, bring her limousine around. Mabel hated to walk anywhere.

"That's not necessary" Hutch said. "The party is just across the Square, and it's a pleasant evening for a walk though the park."

"Very well," Mabel replied. "Let me get my hat."

The trio passed under the nearby Washington Square Arch and entered the park. The walk toward Greenwich Village on the other side of the park was indeed enjoyable. April flowers were beginning to bloom and the night was mild. Even so, Mabel had thrown a mink stole over her flowing red silk dress. "Where is this party?" she asked as they walked.

"It's at the apartment Bea Shostac," Hutch answered, "Big Bill's mistress."

A shiver ran through Mabel at the mention of an illicit IWW love affair. "Is she a revolutionary, like Mr. Haywood?"

Hutch and Neith laughed. "Only in the most discreet way," Hutch said. "Bea Shostac is one of the many young women whom our present system obliges to live what might be called a double life. During the day she is a high school English teacher, where she leads the youth of our country to respect the flag and honor our government. At night she sleeps with Big Bill Haywood when he is in New York, which is seldom nowadays because of the Paterson strike. Many of our brave young American women are adapting themselves in this way to modern life, and thus doing their share towards the final disintegration of society."

Neith laughed at that. "It takes Hutch to see the profound significance of the liaison. Hutchie has to see heroism and rebellion wherever he looks. But I can see why Haywood would be interested in Miss Shostac. She is quite a beautiful young woman."

Bea Shostac's apartment was on a quiet street just outside Washington Square. The trio climbed the stairs and knocked on the door. A young woman answered their knock and welcomed them. They entered and Hutch introduced Mabel to Bea Shostac, the woman who had answered the door. Mabel looked her over and noted that she had the blackest hair Mabel had ever seen, drawn down, Madonna fashion, against the whitest skin she had ever seen. She was, Mabel reluctantly conceded, quite a beautiful young woman.

Mabel looked about the room. It was a small dark apartment, sparsely furnished with only a few chairs for the guests, and lit only by an array of candles burning here and there. Evidently, high school English teachers weren't paid very much. A haze of cigarette smoke created a cloud layer up against the ceiling and a Gramophone was playing the kind of Negro "race music" Mabel knew her friend Carl Van Vechten would have enjoyed. Because of the lack of chairs, the people in the room stood about chatting, or sat together on pillows strewn over the bare wooden floor. One young man rose from his plain wooden chair and offered it to Mabel, who gratefully accepted it.

Hutch and Neith immediately fell into conversation with friends they found there, while Mabel looked over the people in the room. They had noticed Mabel, elegant and attired in flamboyant red silk as she entered the room with Hutch and Neith, but then had returned to their conversations, ignoring her. This peeved Mabel, as she was used to being the center of attention.

It was immediately clear to her which of the people was Big Bill Haywood. He sprawled in one of the few chairs, a great battered hulk of a man with an eminent look about him. His one good eye seemed to have a steady watchfulness. He looked, Mabel thought, like a sturdy old eagle. His arm rested on the shoulders of Bea Shostac, who had returned to his side and was sitting on the floor next to him. Several other young women, whom Mabel presumed to be school teacher friends of Bea's, lolled on the floor around Big Bill, listening to him with rapt attention. His own attention, however, seemed to be directed at one young man sitting on the floor before him, looking up at Big Bill as he described the long silk strike in Paterson.

"You should have seen it, Jack," Big Bill said to the young man. "There's a war going on in Paterson and the endurance and solidarity of these immigrant workers is just amazing. The police have turned into organized gunmen for the bosses. I wish you could have been there for the funeral of Modestino, who was shot by one of the hired gunmen. A great tide of mill hands followed his coffin to the grave and dropped red flowers into it. The grave looked like a pool of blood. Then they marched out of the cemetery singing *The Internationale.* It was absolutely inspiring.

"You should go to Paterson, Jack, and write an article about it for *The Masses.* The strike's been going on for two months now, and we can't get a damned word about it into the New York papers. It's a conspiracy of silence. There is great drama and great tragedy in Paterson, Jack, but very few of our outside comrades know about it.

"Besides, the strike is at a stalemate. The workers are strong and are holding out, but they can't go on forever. A long strike is a lost strike, Jack, and we need allies, and we need them soon, to break the stalemate. We need some way to break through to a larger public. That's why you should go to Paterson and write about it."

Big Bill rambled on, complaining about the lack of publicity the strike was getting in New York. As she listened, Mabel remembered the conversation around her dinner table with MacKaye and Collier about the pageant movement that was spreading across the land. She also remembered her own effort to turn all of Florence into one big Renaissance pageant. And she recalled her recent involvement in the big Armory Show of *avant-garde* art. *That* had certainly garnered a lot of publicity for modern art. Simply everyone talked about nothing else! The solution to Big Bill's conspiracy of silence seemed perfectly obvious to her. She interrupted Big Bill's complaints, saying, "Why don't you just bring the strike to New York and *show* it to your comrades?"

Big Bill turned his one good eye on her. "What do you mean?"

Mabel rushed on. "Why don't you just hire a great hall and re-enact the strike as a pageant right here in New York? Show the whole thing, the closed mills, the police attacks on the picket lines, the gunmen, the murder of the striker, the funeral. And then have all of you strike leaders, you and Tresca and Flynn, give the same speeches that you delivered at the grave in Paterson. It would be great publicity, I'm sure."

For a moment Big Bill said nothing, then he erupted with enthusiasm. "By God! That's a great idea! But, where? What hall would be big enough to tell the whole story of the strike?"

Again, the answer seemed obvious to Mabel. "Why, Madison Square Garden, of course, the biggest hall in New York City! Why not? If it's big enough for Barnum's three-ring circus and Buffalo Bill's Wild West Show, it's certainly big enough to portray your strike."

The audacity of Mabel's idea stunned Big Bill into complete silence. The land where Madison Square Garden stood had originally belonged to a Vanderbilt. Later, J. P. Morgan and Andrew Carnegie developed it and gave the contract to noted architect Stanford White to design and construct the building. White built the Moorish-Venetian-Renaissance-style Madison Square Garden in 1890. With cream-colored brick and terracotta trim, and with Italian arcades, it was one of his proudest achievements. It occupied the entire block between 26th and 27th Streets. It had a rooftop restaurant and garden, whence its name. When completed in 1890, it also had the tallest tower in the city, topped by a nude statue of the Greek goddess Diana, designed by noted sculptor Augustus Saint-Gaudens. Nothing eclipsed that tower until 1913 with the construction of the Woolworth Building downtown, itself a veritable cathedral of capitalism.

Stanford White reserved several floors in his tower for his own use. It was in his apartment in that tower that, at the age of 47, he seduced, or drugged and raped, the 15-year-old Evelyn Nesbit, an aspiring showgirl. Thereafter, for a few years, White supported the teenage Evelyn and her showbiz mother in grand style in exchange for Evelyn being willing to cavort in the tower with him, and beguile him by swinging, bejeweled and nearly nude, on a red velvet swing. White's wealth and privilege allowed him to flaunt his relationship with the teenage girl with impunity, as polite New York society looked the other way.

At the age of 20 Evelyn married Harry K. Thaw, the wealthy heir of a Pittsburgh Robber Baron family. Harry Thaw did not forgive White for seducing, or raping, his young bride, and so, on June 25, 1906, he confronted White in the rooftop restaurant's garden and shot him dead. The idea of staging a workers' strike pageant in Stanford White's edifice was a shocking idea.

But at that moment the young man who had been sitting on the floor listening to Big Bill's account of the Paterson strike jumped up and exclaimed, "By God, that's a wonderful idea! I'll *do* it!"

The crowd erupted into cheers and applause. "Well, if anyone can do it, you can Jack," someone laughed.

The young man rushed over to shake Mabel's hand. "My name's John Reed," he said, pumping her hand energetically. "I'll go to Paterson and look things over. I'll not only write about the strike for *The Masses*, but I'll make a pageant of the strike in Madison Square Garden! I can see the whole thing!"

Already vivid strike tableaux were forming in Reed's mind. It didn't seem to himself to be beyond his reach. In his junior year at Harvard, just a few years before, he had been vice president of the Drama Club. In his senior year he had managed both the Drama Club and the Glee Club. He had been the "Ibis," the second in command of *The Harvard Lampoon,* and wrote lyrics for the annual camp musical presented by Harvard's Hasty Pudding Club. At Harvard's football games he had been a cheerleader, leading hundreds, even thousands, in coordinated cheers for Harvard's crimson warriors. A workers' pageant in Madison Square Garden was simply a little bigger production. He was confident he could pull it off.

Mabel looked the young man over as he shook her hand. He was big and athletic, with a strong broad chest. He had a jutting boxer's chin and a mop of brown hair curling down over his brow. She knew of the radical journalist, John Reed, and had read some of his poems and articles in *The Masses.* She was pleased to see that the man behind the legendary name was such a great handsome figure. He was much more attractive than Big Bill Haywood.

Reed released Mabel's hand and kneeled on the floor next to her. "Where do you live? I'll come and see you as soon as I get back."

Mabel told him her Fifth Avenue address. "I'll come see you the minute I return from Paterson. We'll work this thing out and make it happen! By God! A Paterson strike pageant at Madison Square Garden! Why didn't anyone ever think of this before? It's pure genius!"

Caught up in Reed's enthusiasm, Mabel also became excited at the idea. She glowed with a combination of pride and embarrassment, pleased at Reed's endorsement of her idea. Yes, it was a good idea, she decided, but it was just another instance of the cosmic force of the universe flowing through her and working its will. It was simply meant to be.

She smiled at the handsome young man kneeling next to her as he continued speaking excitedly about the vision of the pageant that was already unfolding in his mind's eye. And perhaps it was also meant to be, she thought, that I come here tonight and meet this beautiful youth. Perhaps that, too, was merely the universe flowing through me and bringing the two of us together to create a pageant. Yes, she thought, her idea for a workers' pageant really was a wonderful idea.

She continued smiling at John Reed as she welcomed and grew accustomed to the idea of them working together. *Que sera, sera*, she thought. What will be, will be.

John Reed in Paterson

John Reed arrived in Paterson by train from New York around six o'clock on the morning of April 28th. If he was going to write about the strike, he felt he needed to find out more about it first-hand. The morning was cold and gray and a light rain was falling. The streets were deserted as he began walking toward the mill district. He soon fell in with workmen walking in the same direction, their hands in their pockets and their collars turned up against the morning chill. Shortly, they reached a long street lined on one side with the silk mills, and on the other by a row of wooden tenement houses. The sidewalks were empty, but groups of policemen with billy clubs were clumped at the mill entrances. Chatting men and women clustered at the windows and doors of the tenement houses, as if waiting for a show to begin.

The show soon began. The workmen who had been walking toward the mills with Reed now began walking back and forth in front of the mill entrances, forming a picket line. The rain continued to fall and it dripped from the hat brims of the parading pickets. Their number slowly grew as more men, young boys, and even a few couples of young men and women walking together joined them. Meanwhile, people began drifting out from the tenement houses across the street and either joined the picket lines or gathered in knots at the street corners. A few men gathered for shelter from the rain under the canopy of a saloon. A policeman approached them and yelled, "Break it up! You can't stand there! Get off the street and go home!" Without protest the men left the shelter of the saloon and drifted off down the street.

On the mill side of the street the marching pickets had grown to few hundred. Then a scab appeared with his tin lunch pail, escorted by two plainclothes detectives. The pickets immediately began deriding the scab with choruses of hoots and boos. The policemen who were clustered around the mill gate moved out to part the picket line and make way for the scab to enter the mill.

Despite the rain and the drab grayness of the sky, the morning grew brighter as the sun struggled to shine through the cloud cover and the number of marching pickets continued to grow. They plodded back and forth before the mill gates, hands in pockets, heads down, rain dripping from their hats. Reed asked a man standing in the open door of his tenement house if he could take shelter from the rain on his porch with three other men already on the porch. The man nodded, and Reed climbed up on the wooden porch.

A patrolling policeman noticed Reed climb up on the porch and came into the yard. The other three men standing with Reed might well have been boarders in the house, but it was clear that the well-dressed Reed, in his suit coat and tie, was not a silk worker. The policeman pointed his club at Reed and yelled at the man in the door. "Does this man live in your house?" The man in the doorway shook his head.

The policeman motioned with his club for Reed to move and yelled at him, "You! Get the hell off that porch!"

"I have the permission of the homeowner to stand on this porch," Reed replied.

"To hell with that! I said get the hell off the porch!"

"I will not."

The policeman jumped onto the porch, grabbed Reed by the upper arm, and forced him off the porch and onto the sidewalk. Another policeman joined them and both cops stood threateningly before Reed. "Now, you move along," the first policemen shouted in Reed's face, "and get the hell off this street."

Reed stood his ground. "I'll do nothing of the sort. I'm an American citizen, and I have a right to stand on this street, or any other street."

The policeman glowered at Reed and thrust his face up close to Reed's. "You move along, or by God, I'll arrest you!"

"Then you'll have to arrest me."

At that both cops grabbed Reed roughly by the arms and marched him quickly along the sidewalk to a waiting patrol wagon. The cops shoved Reed into the back of it and slammed the door shut. The patrol wagon then took off with a loud clanging of gongs, roaring down the street with Reed bouncing around inside. As it rushed along the rows of marching pickets, ragged cheers went up and some of the pickets waved.

At the police station the policemen jerked Reed rudely out of the back of the wagon and hustled him inside. His police escort halted him before a police sergeant seated behind a desk. "What's the charge?" the sergeant asked Reed's arresting officer.

"Loitering," the officer answered.

The sergeant looked at Reed, taking note of his fine clothes and obviously "American" look. "What's your name?"

"John Reed."

The sergeant wrote the name in his ledger book. "What's your occupation?"

Reed drew himself up proudly. "Poet," he answered.

The sergeant looked up from his ledger and glared at Reed, but dutifully wrote "Poet" in his book.

"OK, lock him up," the sergeant said, and gestured over his shoulder.

Reed's police escort shoved him towards the back of the station and through a door into a corridor lined on both sides by jail cells. The cells were already jammed with workmen, who stood at the bars, curious to see who the new arrival might be. They didn't recognize Reed, but they immediately broke into loud cheering and clapping at the sight of him. Reed's police escort opened the door to one cell and pushed him inside, then slammed the door and locked it.

Reed looked around the cell. It was about four feet wide and seven feet long. Two iron bunks, one above the other, hung by chains from one wall. The bunks were bare, with no bedding or pillows on them. The floor was slimy with scum and, in one corner, there was an even slimier toilet with no lid. There were two men already in the cell. One was a Negro, sitting on the lower iron bunk. The other, standing in the middle of the cell, was a large swarthy man with a moustache and a Van Dyke beard, just as well dressed as Reed. Both eyed Reed with curiosity. Reed thrust out his hand to the standing man. "I'm John Reed," he said, "just in from New York."

The large man, his hands grasping the lapels of his suit coat, did not reach for Reed's outstretched hand. He just stared at Reed silently. Finally, he spoke. "Tresca," he said. "Carlo Tresca." Then he spat on the filthy floor near Reed's shoes and continued to stare at Reed.

"I've heard of you," Reed said.

"I not hear of you," Tresca replied.

Realizing Tresca was not going to shake his hand, Reed extended his hand to the Negro sitting on the bunk. The Negro jumped up and eagerly shook Reed's hand. "You can have my bunk," he said, indicating the bed.

"No, no," Reed replied. "I wouldn't think of it. It's your bed, I'll just stand here."

The Negro sat back down on the bed, and Tresca sat beside him. Reed leaned against the cell wall. The Negro was willing to chat with Reed, but Tresca rebuffed every effort Reed made to engage him in conversation. The most Reed could get out of him were grunts. Meanwhile, the noise from the other cells, crammed with up to a dozen men each, was deafening, as the prisoners yelled, sang, and chanted IWW slogans.

A little later the outside door opened and a large group of pickets were shoved in. At their appearance, pandemonium broke out in the jail cells, with the prisoners in each cell cheering and slamming their iron bunks against the metal walls of their cells. The repeated slamming of the bunks against the walls sounded like cannons booming on a battlefield. The new arrivals were crammed into the already full cells, and suddenly there were half a dozen men standing in Reed's small cell.

Then everyone in the holding cells began cheering even louder. "Hooray for the One Big Union!" yelled one voice. Every voice in the cells answered with a unanimous and deafening response, "Hooray for the One Big Union!"

The call and response then continued: "Hooray for the IWW!" "Hooray for Big Bill!" "Hooray for the strike!" "To hell with the cops!" "To hell with the mayor!" "To hell with the AFL!" Everyone in Reed's cell, including the Negro, Carlo Tresca, and Reed himself, joined in the cheers, which continued to the accompaniment of slamming bunk beds.

Eventually the outside door opened again and a squadron of policemen entered and began opening all the cell doors, hurrying the inmates outside. The inmates left cheering, and Reed could hear the cheers of others outside the police station greeting them. The men in Reed's cell also began cheering. "What's going on?" Reed asked one of them.

"The county jail is full," he said. "There's no more room for strikers. We're being released." Reed smiled at that.

A policeman opened the door to Reed's cell and his companions began filing out, laughing and cheering. Carlo Tresca, however, remained sitting on the lower bunk. As Reed approached the cell door, the policeman shoved him back into the cell. "Not you," he said. "You stay!" Then he slammed and locked the cell door and followed the cheering workers out. Reed heard the cheers of the departing strikers fading away.

Reed turned to Tresca. "What's going on?"

Tresca merely shrugged, and said nothing.

And so Reed and Tresca waited in the now silent cellblock, saying nothing to each other.

Later that morning a squad of policemen came for the both of them and escorted them out of the police station and into a patrol wagon, which took off with much clanging of gongs. After a short while the wagon stopped and the two men were pulled out of the back of the wagon and separated. Two policemen gripped Reed's arms and hurried him into a small courtroom, where they stood him before the podium of Passaic County Recorder James Carroll. To John Reed it seemed this magistrate had a cruel and merciless face, and he expected the worst.

"What's the charge?" Recorder Carroll asked.

"Loitering," a policeman said.

"How do you plead?" Recorder Carroll asked Reed.

"Not guilty," Reed answered, and prepared to explain his situation.

Recorder Carroll slammed his gavel down on a wood block in front of him and cut Reed off. "Guilty! Twenty days in the county jail! Next!"

Before he could object, two policemen grabbed Reed's arms and hurried him out of the courtroom. They hustled him back into the patrol wagon for another clanging ride, this one longer. It ended at the Passaic County Jail, a large, damp, filthy, rat-infested building dating from the Civil War. There Reed's personal possessions were taken away and he was ordered to strip. He was forced to bathe in a small tin tub filled with cold and scummy water. Next he was given a prison uniform to wear, consisting of a faded blue cotton shirt, dirty gray pants, and a canvas coat.

Then he was thrust into a long dark corridor lined with cells stacked one row on top of the other three tiers high. The only light was a small ceiling skylight at the top of a funnel shaped airshaft. The cells were already packed with inmates, all of them wearing the identical three-piece prison uniform Reed wore. Reed noted that there was none of the cheering and singing that had greeted Reed back at the Paterson police station's holding cells.

He was shoved into a cell with several other inmates, all Italians who spoke no English. Reed's attempts at communication were met only with incomprehension. The pale daylight filtering in from the skylight eventually faded and night came on. As he stretched out on his iron bunk that night, with the sound of snoring men around him, John Reed contemplated his day. So much had changed in just 24 hours! He'd awakened that morning in his soft warm bed in his apartment on Washington Square. Now he was trying to sleep on a cold iron bunk in a filthy jail cell in another state, jammed in with men who didn't even speak English. And he had three weeks of this ahead of him! It was hard for him to actually believe this could happen in America. Then, thinking such thoughts, he drifted off to sleep.

The next morning the prisoners were released from their cells to mingle in the large common room. Reed wandered among them, seeking someone to speak to about the strike. He noticed Carlo Tresca in the crowd, now dressed in the same drab prison uniform as Reed. He eagerly approached him, but Tresca turned his back on him and refused to speak to him. The other prisoners seemed to be a mélange of Italian strikers and common criminals. Some seemed to be mere boys. One of them Reed discovered to be seventeen and had been in that hellhole for nine months, although he had never been convicted of any crime. One of them wandered around in the crowd screaming incoherently in an ululating voice, seemingly insane. The prisoners ignored him. Other prisoners gathered in twos and threes, speaking furtively and eyeing Reed with suspicion.

Then the main door clanged open and two policemen ushered in Big Bill Haywood, minus his Stetson hat, but still in his street clothes. A shout erupted from the prisoners and they clustered eagerly around Big Bill, bombarding him with questions in a wild cacophony of voices. Reed hurried over to join those crowding around the Wobbly leader.

Big Bill saw him, and a smile broke out on his rugged face. "Well, Jack, I told you to come to Paterson, but I didn't tell you to get arrested!" He put his arm around Reed, grabbing him by the shoulder, and pulled him close, hugging him to his massive chest. That broke the ice, and the Italian strikers who had previously avoided him now smiled at Reed and gathered around him.

Feeling welcome at last, Reed smiled and shook hands with all those thrust out to shake his. He looked up at Big Bill and said, "And I didn't expect to see you in this place, Bill."

Big Bill laughed loudly. "It's an occupational hazard, Jack. I'm used to it."

Then Big Bill spied Carlo Tresca and called him over. "Carlo, I want you to meet Jack Reed. He writes for *The Masses,* and he's on our side."

Tresca came over, grinned a big smile at Reed and, this time, offered Reed his hand. Reed shook it gladly. "We meet yesterday," Tresca said to Big Bill. He continued smiling at Reed as he pumped his hand. "You no worker, so I think maybe you a police spy. I no trust you. Now I trust you!"

"Boys," Big Bill said in a loud voice to those crowding around him, "this man is a reporter and I can vouch for him. He's OK, and he wants to tell our side of the story. You tell him everything about the strike."

After that, the men were eager to speak with Reed, and answered all his questions as best they could. Some of them were in jail for "loitering," like Reed. Others were charged with "unlawful assembly." Some others had simply been standing in a group at a railroad crossing, waiting for the train to pass so they could go home after picketing. The police came upon them and arrested them all for "rioting." Recorder Carroll had sentenced them to six months in the county jail.

Yet all of them, Italians, Jews, Poles, Lithuanians, all remained defiant, ready to curse their jailers and eager to return to the picket lines. There was among the prisoners one "free born" Englishman, as he described himself. He told Reed he was there for insulting a mill foreman who had come out of the mill and ordered him away from the mill gate, where he was picketing. "I put the curse of Cromwell on him," the Englishman said, "and the coppers grabbed me right off."

Others told Reed how all the religious leaders in Paterson, both Catholic and Protestant, and even most of the rabbis, were against the strike and urged them to go back to work. The Reverend William A. Littell, pastor of the Presbyterian Church, routinely flayed Big Bill Haywood, Carlo Tresca, and Elizabeth Gurley Flynn in his sermons and advised the workers to be respectful and obedient to their employers. The saloons were the true cause of their unhappiness, Reverend Littell told them, not the mill owners.

"Doesn't that make you angry?" Reed asked the strikers. "Don't you wish you were back outside, on the picket lines, part of the struggle?"

"We part of the struggle in here," they told him. "We stay here. Fill up the damn jail. Pretty soon no more room. Pretty soon can't arrest no more pickets!"

One young Italian showed Reed a newspaper with three stories about the strike. He pointed to the headlines of the three stories in turn. "You a reporter," he said. "Explain these to me."

Reed looked at the headlines. "American Federation of Labor hopes to break the strike next week," said one. "Newark Socialists refuse to help Paterson strikers," said another. The third read, "Victor Berger says, 'I am a member of the AFL and I have no love for the IWW in Paterson.'"

"I no understand," the Italian said to Reed, "so you tell me. Socialist, he say, 'Workmen of the world, unite!' AFL, he say, 'All workmen join together.' Both these groups, he say, 'I am for the working class.' All right, I say, I am the working class. I unite. I strike. I Socialist. I belong union. I strike with IWW. Then Socialist, AFL, he say, 'No! You *cannot* unite! You *cannot* strike!' I no understand. You explain me."

Reed felt at a loss to explain the nuances of the infighting among the rival organizations. All he could say was, "Well, it seems the Socialist Party and the American Federation of Labor have forgotten all about the class struggle. All we can do is say, 'To hell with them,' and stand strong with the IWW."

The Italian worker smiled at Reed. "Yes," he said. "We stand strong with IWW. You and me, and IWW, together we stand strong."

Reed nodded. "Yes," he agreed. "You and me. Together we stand strong with the IWW."

And, saying that, John Reed seemed to reach a revelation in his own mind. Yes, he thought, the Socialist Party and the AFL, they're both useless. They really have forgotten all about the class struggle. These poor brave guys here are fighting a desperate battle against long odds. They need all the help they can get. And those so-called champions of the working class are standing by with folded arms doing nothing. Worse, they're on the side of the bosses against the IWW, the only group out there fighting for these workers. By God! I was only playing at revolution when I proclaimed the Republic of Greenwich Village on top of the Washington Arch. But this is the real thing! This is the real revolution!

He looked around at all the immigrant workingmen crowded into the jail with him, the Italians, the Poles, the Russian Jews. They're locked up in here simply because they want better lives for themselves and their families. They want what everyone wants, a chance to live, a chance to breathe free. That's why they came to America. Isn't that what America is supposed to be all about?

And, Reed asked himself, what do they get once they get here? They're starved and beaten, worked to death for a handful of pennies, and jailed when they protest. But, despite that, they still protest. They sing their union songs, and denounce their jailers and their bosses, and they're ready to return to the picket lines as soon as they get out. *They* are the real leaders of this strike, Reed thought, not Big Bill, or Carlo Tresca, or Elizabeth Gurley Flynn. Hell, they *are* the strike!

Reed felt suddenly unworthy to be among such men. At the same time, however, he felt proud to be among them, proud that they accepted him on a basis of equality as a comrade in the same struggle, despite his different background, despite coming from Harvard and Greenwich Village. His heart went out to them, and he vowed he would prove worthy of their trust.

Four days later Jessie Ashley, the main IWW attorney working in Paterson, obtained the release of Big Bill Haywood, Carlo Tresca, and John Reed. The strikers crowded around the three as they prepared to leave. "Don't forget about us," they implored the three.

"You know we won't," Big Bill assured them. "You're in here for us, and we will be out there for you. It doesn't matter if we're on a picket line or in a jail cell, we're all part of the same struggle."

That's right, Reed said to himself, thinking of all the nationalities and religions jammed together in the prison, thinking of the Negro with whom he had first shared his cell. No matter who we are, foreign born or native born, black or white or some other color; no matter where we are, in jail or out; no matter what we're doing, in Paterson, or Greenwich Village, or anywhere else, we're all part of the same struggle.

"Too bad you get in jail," they said to Reed as he prepared to leave. "You not belong here. Now you go out, you tell our story."

"Yes, I will," Reed assured them. "I promise. I will tell your story."

The Pageant or The Picket Lines?

  Mabel Dodge lived on Fifth Avenue just north of the Washington Square Arch. She had chosen the address deliberately. It was good and fitting to live on Fifth Avenue. The best people lived on Fifth Avenue. Opposite Fifth Avenue's St. Patrick's Cathedral the gold baron Darius Ogden Mills had paid the highest price ever paid for land in Manhattan and constructed a fabulous pleasure palace worthy of Kubla Khan. California baron Collis Huntington, lord of the Southern Pacific Railroad, built a huge multi-million dollar mansion on Fifth Avenue at Fifty-Seventh Street, adjacent to the palace of William C. Whitney, who'd married a Standard Oil heiress -- but then Huntington never bothered to move into it. The palace of William H. Vanderbilt, in the "Greek Renaissance" style with imported marble and which took two years to build, and the adjoining one of his daughter, extended for a full block along Fifth Avenue from Fifth-First to Fifth-Second Street. It was filled with medieval armor, Renaissance tapestries, and paintings by Old Masters whose names he could hardly pronounce. Along with the neighboring French chateau of William Kissam Vanderbilt, the bright lights from their windows turned the night along Fifth Avenue into brilliant day. Mabel's apartment at 23 Fifth Avenue couldn't compete with such opulence, but she was in the right neighborhood.

  Early on the morning of May 3rd, John Reed began pounding on the door to Mabel's apartment. Vittorio, Mabel's butler, answered the pounding. In the hallway outside he saw a disheveled and haggard-looking young man panting from running up the stairs to Mabel's apartment. Vittorio leveled a look of withering disdain at the unexpected visitor. "May I help you?" he said.

  "I'm John Reed. I've come to see Mabel Dodge," the young man said.

  "Mrs. Dodge is not awake at this hour," Vittorio replied. "Nor does she receive unannounced strangers."

  "I'm not a stranger. She knows me and she's expecting me. Please announce me."

  Vittorio looked Reed over dubiously. "Very well, Mr. Reed," he finally said, stepping aside and gesturing for Reed to enter. "You may come in and wait while I announce you."

  Reed entered the apartment and Vittorio, as he disappeared into the depths of the apartment, left him in the large room facing out on Fifth Avenue. Reed had never been to one of Mabel's salons, and so he was seeing it for the first time. He looked around the room, taking in the huge marble fireplace, the white bearskin on the floor in front of it, the Italian furnishings, and the Venetian chandelier. He whistled softly in appreciation.

  Then Vittorio returned, with Mabel Dodge herself close behind. She looked sleepy and confused and was swathed in diaphanous silk. Reed couldn't tell if it was a dress or her nightgown. "Mr. Reed," Mabel said. "This is certainly unexpected. You look somewhat distraught."

  Reed smiled and walked toward her. "I've had a long night, but I told you I'd come see you as soon as I returned from Paterson."

  "You went to Paterson?"

  "Yes, I was in jail there, with the strikers. Now I've come to talk to you about the pageant."

"The pageant? You're serious?"

"More serious than ever. Aren't you?"

"It was just an idea."

"It was a wonderful idea. And after spending some time in jail with the strikers, I'm more convinced than ever that the pageant must be produced."

Mabel considered the handsome young man standing before her. She had certainly been impressed with him when she met him at Bea Shostac's apartment, and she had been flattered that he had praised her pageant idea and said he would go to Paterson to research it, but people say many things that never come to pass.

"Well, Mr. Reed," she said, "I would certainly like to hear about how you ended up in jail in Paterson. Why don't we sit, and you can tell me about it, and we can discuss the pageant."

Reed enjoyed talking about his adventures, especially to appreciative female audiences. He smiled, and made an awkward, almost imperceptible bow. "Call me Jack, and I'd love to tell you about it. You'll find it hard to believe."

"I'm sure I will," Mable replied, and she asked Vittorio to bring in some coffee for the two of them. Then she directed Reed to the front room where they could sit comfortably. Bright spring sunlight lit up the room. Mabel selected two comfortable stuffed chairs for them and Vittorio soon wheeled in a cart with a steaming pot of coffee and exquisite china cups on saucers. He poured two cups of coffee, offered them cream and sugar, and then left them alone.

And then John Reed told Mabel Dodge about Paterson. He had just returned from Paterson and had not slept the night before. Instead, he had worked all through the night at his typewriter in his apartment on the other side of Washington Square, pecking furiously at the keys, pounding out an account of his visit to Paterson for *The Masses*. Max Eastman had assured him that if Reed gave him a story immediately, he could get it in the June issue of the magazine. And so, in a fever, Reed wrote about the war in Paterson. Then he had rushed the manuscript over to Max's apartment just that morning.

Now he told Mabel about what he had written, about the workers plodding in the rain on their picket lines; about the police shouting at them and threatening them with their clubs; about being arrested because he refused to get off the street. And he told her about his days and nights in the cold, stinking, and crowded cells of the Paterson police station and the Passaic County Jail.

And he told her how Carlo Tresca and Big Bill Haywood stood among the workers in jail and gave them hope and encouragement. And he told her of how the immigrant workers, the Italians, Jews, Poles, and Lithuanians, sang and cheered and called each other brothers, how they welcomed him into their company, and how they vowed to go on fighting, no matter how long the struggle lasted. And he told Mabel how he had promised the workers, when he was released, that he would tell their story, so that the whole world knew of their sacrifices and their bravery.

"And that's why there has to be a pageant," Reed concluded. "The world has to know this story, and we have to tell it."

Mabel had listened to Reed's story with rapt attention. It all seemed so exotic and alien to her, far beyond her experience. She was caught up in Reed's telling, and felt she could see the workers in jail, could smell the stench of their cells, hear their songs. And she felt herself responding even more to the enthusiasm of John Reed than she had at Bea Shostac's apartment. The way he looked into her eyes with a fierce intensity as he told his story thrilled her, and she felt a pleasurable warmth at his need for her. She reached out and laid her hand on his. He did not draw back.

"You're quite right," she said. "We have to tell this amazing story. What do you want me to do?"

"You suggested Madison Square Garden for a pageant," Reed said. "You need to reserve it. You're the only one who can do it. You have the name and the connections."

Mabel considered that. "Yes, I could do that. But they would want some assurances. I have a certain amount of money, but I could not pay for the rental myself."

"We will form a committee to deal with that," Reed said. "You just make the reservation. I have my own contacts. I know organizers and artists. We'll pull in people from the unions. I'll organize everything." Reed placed his other hand on top of Mabel's and let it rest there. "Together, we can do this!"

Mabel smiled at Reed, catching his enthusiasm. She looked deeply into his eyes. She was sure something magical and magnetic was passing between her and Reed. "Yes, I'm sure we can, Jack," she finally said. "We can do this… together."

****

"We can't do this," Elizabeth Gurley Flynn said. "It's a distraction from the strike. The strike is at a critical moment, and we can't spare any workers from the picket lines. First and foremost, we have to keep the mills shut down."

"You've said yourself the mills are shut down tight as a vacuum," Big Bill responded. "We have thousands on the picket lines. Some can be spared for a pageant."

"Yes," Carlo Tresca said, "we have many on the picket lines, but a strike needs constant action, like a man needs air to breathe. That's why we can't stop the picketing, the rallies. We have to keep up the energy, and the passion."

The three of them were sitting in a back room of IWW Local 152 in Paterson. John Reed had told Big Bill that Mabel Dodge was approaching Madison Square Garden for a pageant date. Now Big Bill was trying to enlist the backing of his IWW colleagues in Paterson. But Gurley Flynn and Carlo Tresca were resisting the idea. Big Bill continued arguing with his comrades in his slow, patient way.

"First, we're not talking about ending the picketing," Big Bill said. "That goes on. But, we have 25,000 workers out on strike, 95% of the workforce, and the mills are completely closed down, and have been for over two months. So we don't need 20,000 marchers on the picket lines everyday. We can spare maybe 1,000 of them, 500 men and 500 women, for a pageant.

"Second," Big Bill continued, "the same activity, the picketing and rallies, can only go on for so long. In the beginning, people are enthusiastic, they are eager to march and rally and show their solidarity. But, after a while, they're not so eager to crawl out of bed at six o'clock on a cold rainy morning to go plodding in the soaking rain until a policeman comes along and clubs them or arrests them. They say, 'Let someone else do it just for today,' and they roll over and go back to sleep. The strike is over two months old, now. All the drama of continuous involvement is building up an immunity to any further excitement. Enthusiasm is beginning to lag, that's what you're concerned about. Any tactic, like picketing and rallies, that goes on too long becomes boring, no matter how much one believes in the strike. We have to do something different to maintain the strikers' morale and enthusiasm."

"We can bring in different speakers," Flynn replied. "We can get some well-known people to come and encourage the strikers."

"We've done that. We brought in Upton Sinclair. We even got Debs to come, even though he's a Socialist. We've run out of big names we can bring in to speak, and, besides, the workers are becoming used to that. But, you're right. The strike is at a critical moment. We can all feel it. It's not going to be the quick victory we had last year in Lawrence. It's important that a strike not be carried on over too long a time. Time is the enemy, and we all know that a long strike is a lost strike. This strike has been going on a long time. We need to do something different."

"That is so," Tresca replied, "it is a long strike. But we just need to keep the pressure on for a little longer. I think we're on the edge of winning."

"Carlo is right," Flynn said. "The workers can win this strike if we just keep up the pressure for a little longer."

"The problem, though," Big Bill said, "is that picketing and rallies are terminal tactics. They become ends in themselves. They don't escalate the pressure. We have to keep escalating the pressure; we can't just keep doing the same things over and over. That becomes a dead end. We have to do something different to increase the pressure."

"And we need to bring in allies," Big Bill continued. "The workers are too weak to win by themselves. If that were true, we would have won the strike by now, like we did in Lawrence. But we're at a stalemate, and the workers just don't have the resources to hold out much longer. Pretty soon, if we don't do something dramatic to escalate the pressure, the solid front we've got here is going to crack. The men can bear to see their wives and kids go hungry for only so long. They're going to begin to settle mill by mill. Then, once some of the strikers go back to work, everything will crumble pretty quickly, and there will be a rush to settle. Those who don't will be blacklisted, and never work again. You know that's what will happen."

Big Bill fell silent and let that sink in. Flynn and Tresca looked at each other. They were just as experienced in strikes as Big Bill. They knew he was right. Solidarity and idealism would take you only so far. If the strike didn't take a dramatic turn, if it continued to drag on the way it was, the men would begin to settle mill by mill, and the strike would soon be lost.

Big Bill decided to push his advantage. "Besides increasing the pressure, a good tactic is also one that people enjoy," he said. "That's why we sing on the picket lines and at the rallies. That's why we bring in interesting speakers. We knew this in Lawrence when we said, yes, we want bread, but we want roses, too! People hunger for more than just bread. They also hunger for drama and adventure, for a breath of life in a dreary, drab existence. That's what they got in the first days and weeks of this strike, but now that drama and adventure is getting old. We need a new drama, a new adventure, to keep the morale up. That's what the pageant will do.

"And it will also give us the allies we need. We've all agreed there's a press blackout in New York, a conspiracy of silence about the strike. If we take the strike itself to New York City, and have the workers themselves present the story of the strike on the largest stage in the city, it will be front-page news in every newspaper. Everyone will know about the strike, every *worker* in the city will know about the strike. And we will win the new allies we need to win this strike."

Elizabeth Gurley Flynn and Carlo Tresca listened to Big Bill's arguments in silence. They were used to picket lines and rallies. That's what had won the Lawrence strike. But the strike in Paterson was dragging on too long. They knew they had to do something dramatic to keep up morale and increase the pressure on the bosses. They had to do something to break the stalemate. They weren't sure a strike pageant in New York City was the right thing to do, but they didn't have any better ideas.

"Who would organize this pageant?" Flynn asked. "You're talking about a giant spectacle on the biggest stage in New York. If it fails, it would be a giant public disaster for the strike and the strikers' morale. All of us, the IWW and the workers, would be a big laughing stock. It's a big gamble. It could lose us the strike."

"There would be an organizing committee in New York, but John Reed is going to mainly organize it. He has the experience doing such things, and he has the contacts among the artists of Greenwich Village to stage the whole thing."

Flynn looked at Tresca, and shrugged her shoulders. He looked back, and shrugged his, as well.

"Very well," Flynn said reluctantly to Big Bill. "If the Central Strike Committee agrees to go along with your idea, we will also. What do you want us to do?"

Down the Stairs

Margaret Sanger's uptown Manhattan apartment was jammed with a motley assortment of Bohemia's denizens: socialists, IWWs, union members, suffragists, poets, playwrights, artists, and theater people of various types. They sat on the few chairs, sat crosslegged on the floor, or stood leaning against the walls. Margaret Sanger had put her children to bed and was sitting at the dining room table, which was cluttered with a scattering of papers. Big Bill Haywood sat in one of the few comfortable chairs, his hand stroking the upper arm of Bea Shostac, who sat on the floor next to him. Some of her school teacher girlfriends sat on the floor with her. A haze of cigarette smoke drifted up to the ceiling of the hot and stuffy apartment. Everyone was talking at once, and the noisy buzz of numerous conversations made it hard for anyone to hear what the person sitting in front of them, almost shouting to be heard, was actually saying. John Reed, who seemed to have a personal connection to everyone there, had pulled them all together. In doing so, his manic enthusiasm for his new pageant project had come to infect them all to one degree or another.

Finally, Reed stepped up on an ottoman footstool, clapped his hands together loudly, and spoke in his stentorian cheerleader's voice, "People, people! This meeting of the Paterson Strike Committee will now come to order!"

The buzz ceased, but one voice, that of Village anarchist Hippolyte Havel, quickly objected, "I thought this was a meeting of the Pageant Committee?" There was a Pageant Executive Committee, serving as the umbrella committee overseeing the progress of several work committees. It was comprised of John Reed and Mabel Dodge, as well as Big Bill Haywood, Margaret Sanger, and Jessie Ashley, the elderly radical attorney who had gotten Big Bill, Tresca, and John Reed out of the Passaic County Jail. She had a maiden aunt demeanor, and was called upon ceaselessly in labor struggles for her legal expertise. Someone with that expertise was needed on the Pageant Executive Committee.

"Hippie, the Pageant is an extension of the strike," Reed answered. "Our purpose is to bring the strike to New York City; to let the workers themselves tell the story of their strike, and by doing so gain more publicity and support for their strike, thereby increasing pressure on the bosses. So, for all intents and purposes, this is a strike meeting."

"The Pageant will also raise funds for the strike, will it not?" asked Walter Lippmann, also occupying one of the few chairs in the apartment. Lippmann was a classmate of Reed's, and had been founder and president of the Harvard Socialist Club while a student in Cambridge. Shortly after graduation he had worked as an advisor to George Lunn and his Socialist Party colleagues, who had won every office in Schenectady, New York in the November, 1911, municipal elections. After taking office in 1912, however, the Schenectady Socialists, used to being in the opposition, had no idea what to do next. They had called upon the young Lippmann, just out of Harvard and already a rising star in Socialist politics, to advise them on what municipal socialism might look like.

It had been a disillusioning experience for Lippmann. He concluded that the Socialists were intellectually impoverished and had absolutely no idea what to do with political power once they'd won it. There was, he said, a mental aimlessness behind the revolutionary rhetoric of the Socialist Party. There was nothing solid there. It was all bluster and hot air. Indeed, they were so bereft of ideas and plans that, Lippmann said, "They had no idea that they even should have had plans for what to do once they took power."

After two months in Schenectady, Lippmann resigned in disgust as Mayor Lunn's adviser. However, he still thought of himself as a socialist, and was looking around for some organization to believe in. For this reason, he was willing to give Big Bill and the IWW a chance to prove themselves. That was why he came, and why he was willing to support the Pageant by writing about it for the newspapers.

After listening to his skeptical questions in several meetings, however, Mabel Dodge had decided that Lippmann's support only went so far. Disdainfully comparing Lippmann to Big Bill Haywood, Mabel concluded, "That man will certainly never lose an eye fighting on the barricades."

"Walter, let's put an end to that kind of thinking right now," Reed said, responding to Lippmann's question. "The Pageant is a one-shot performance. Even if we sell out Madison Square Garden, there is no way we can make a profit. The expenses are just too big. We'll be lucky if we don't lose our shirts. The purpose of the Pageant is publicity for the strike, pure and simple. That publicity may then generate financial support for the strike down the road in donations, but to think of the Pageant itself as a fundraiser is to set us up for a big disappointment. It's just not possible."

Lippmann nodded. "OK, Jack, I just wanted to be clear on that."

"OK," Reed said, "Now what I want to do right now is get progress reports from our various work committees. Mabel, here, was able to secure a date for the Pageant at Madison Square Garden. It's June 7th, only three weeks away. The Pageant Executive Committee has already signed the contract and given them a $250 check for the deposit, which very generously came from Mabel. Now we have a tremendous amount of work to do in three weeks, so we have to stay focused and stay busy."

Reed looked around at the group, thinking. Then he continued, "By the way, Mabel, who is also on the publicity committee, has also managed to get us our first notice in the papers." Reed grabbed a copy of that day's *New York Times* from the clutter on Sanger's dining room table and held it up for all to see. There was an interview in it with Mabel. The reporter had asked Mabel, as a member of the Pageant's Executive Committee, the purpose of the Pageant. Mabel told the reporter that, "The Pageant was arranged because the newspapers have never let the people get a fair impression of the IWW. The actors in the pageant will bring out the fact that the IWW is made up of the workers themselves. No such spectacle, presenting in dramatic form the class war raging in society, has ever been staged in America."

"Let's give Mabel a hand," Reed said, and led the group in applause for Mabel's coup. "I couldn't have said it better." Mabel blushed and smiled slightly, acknowledging the applause. She was pleased that Reed was impressed with her publicity work, and had called attention to it.

As the applause died down, Reed continued, "But we also need to give Mabel a hand in publicizing the Pageant in every way we can. We need to talk up the Pageant in our unions, in other organizations that we're members of, to all our friends and acquaintances."

"Also," Reed continued, "Bobby here has designed a poster for the Pageant. Bobby, could you stand up and show us your poster?"

Robert Edmond Jones nodded and stood up to unroll and show his Pageant poster. Like Walter Lippmann, Jones was also a classmate of Reed's from Harvard, where they had become close friends while both were members of the Harvard Drama Club. Also, like Reed, Bobby Jones had moved to New York after graduation to launch his career. In Bobby's case, it was in theater design.

However, he had not been as lucky as Reed in establishing himself. Reed's luck had been in having the famous muckraking journalist Lincoln Steffens as a friend of his father. Once in New York, Steffens took the young Reed under his wing and prevailed upon his friends at *The American*, a well-established general interest magazine, to give Reed a job as a minor editor. In theory, at least, Reed still had that job, but it was mostly a sinecure. He was absent from the magazine's office more than he was present. But, the job paid his share of the rent at the modest apartment at 42 Washington Square South. It also allowed him to spend time on his myriad passion projects, such as being an unpaid member of the editorial collective at *The Masses*, or mounting the Pageant.

Bobby Jones, however, had not had a patron like Lincoln Steffens, who could procure for him a no-show job. One day Reed stumbled across Bobby Jones as he wandered up and down Broadway trying to break into the theater as a designer. Jones was dressed in shabby clothes and looked hungry and gaunt. Reed learned that he was, in fact, penniless and sleeping on the streets. Reed took him back home with him to Washington Square and gave him Alan Seeger's room. Seeger was another Harvard classmate and, like Reed, a budding poet, although his poetry was much better than Reed's. Seeger had departed to write poetry on the Left Bank in Paris, so his room was empty. Then Reed took up a collection from other Harvard classmates of them both to feed and clothe Jones, as well as arrange contacts in the theatrical world.

Now Jones was repaying his debt to Reed by working for him on the Pageant. He had designed a set for the huge 200-foot-long Madison Square Garden stage, a stage big enough for a thousand strikers to appear on it at the same time. He also conceived of the idea of having a wide central aisle down the middle of the audience for the strike re-enactors to use. The strikers would enter from the back of the hall and proceed down the central aisle on their way to the mills. The aisle would also be the street down which the strikers, as mourners, would carry the casket of Valentino Modestino on their way to the cemetery. This would essentially turn the audience into participants, as if watching the funeral procession pass on the streets of Paterson.

Now Bobby Jones showed the gathering the poster he had designed for the Pageant. It portrayed a gigantic worker climbing out of a Paterson silk mill with his arm upraised. It looked dramatic. The people in the room burst into applause as Bobby turned this way and that to display the poster.

"We're going to have thousands of these posters printed up," Reed said. "We need to have them plastered up all over New York. We need to have a committee just in charge of that, to find and coordinate a volunteer poster team."

Then Reed looked over the room and spied John Sloan, the artist friend who had proclaimed the Republic of Greenwich Village with him from atop the Washington Square Arch back in January. "Meanwhile," Reed said, "Sloan here is in the process of painting a huge portrayal of a Paterson silk mill on the Garden stage. The workers will enter the mill through a central gate of the painting, and then pour out of the mill once the strike starts. This painting will be the backdrop for all the action of the strike, the picketing, the confrontations with the police, the funeral of Modestino. Sloan needs helpers down at the Garden to work on painting that backdrop."

Reed paused for a moment, thinking. "Oh, and we need a committee to work on the big IWW signs. We're going to have giant electric images of the letters IWW on the four outside walls of the Garden tower. This is the tallest tower in the city. The night of the performance we're going to plug them in and the letters, 'IWW,' are going to light up the night over Manhattan." Reed smiled at the image in his mind's eye. "It's going to be magnificent." The motley group in the room cheered and burst into another round of applause.

Then Reed looked over at Big Bill, sitting silently on the edge of the group, content to let Reed run the show. "In the orchestra pit, providing music for the Pageant, we're going to have an IWW band. Big Bill is in charge of recruiting the band. The IWW likes to sing, and it has many members who are musicians, so Big Bill says he'll bring them in. The strikers will also bring in their own 26-piece band to march down the center aisle.

"That reminds me," Reed continued. "We also need to reserve a train to bring the strikers in from Paterson on the day of the Pageant. And we need volunteers to canvas florists for donations of red carnations for Modestino's coffin. So, as you can see, there's a lot of work to do, and very little time in which to do it, only 21 days. Everybody needs to pitch in and help in any way they can to get the Garden ready for the performance, and to publicize the Pageant."

Reed ran his hand through his thick head of unruly hair and looked at the floor, momentarily distracted, trying to think of anything he'd forgotten. There was so much that needed to be done that he felt both overwhelmed and energized by the amount of work needed to pull off the Pageant. He hadn't slept except in snatches for days, and was whirling from one aspect of the project to the next in a fever frenzy. Sometimes he felt he couldn't think straight at all, and he was constantly afraid that he'd overlooked something important. At times he felt he might break under the pressure.

"In the meantime," he finally said, "I'm commuting back and forth from New York to Paterson, spending every day in Paterson rehearsing the workers for the performance itself. After the Central Strike Committee approved participation in the Pageant, there was no problem in recruiting volunteers for the performance. The workers were eager to participate. Every day we've got a thousand workers rehearsing the set pieces of the strike in Paterson's Turn Hall. One of the picket captains, a young girl named Hannah Silverman, is in charge of the rehearsals when I'm not there. The Paterson workers are doing their part to get ready, and we here in New York have to do our part."

John Reed paused to let that sink in. The members of the group nodded in silent agreement. Then he continued once more. "However, there is one big problem that has emerged. New York City Sheriff Julius Harburger has banned the singing of both *The Internationale* and *The Marseillaise*. He'll have a big police presence at the Pageant. He has vowed that the minute the strikers or the audience begin singing either song, he'll shut us down. Of course, the strikers are always singing those songs in Paterson, and singing them has to be a big part of the Pageant. There's no way we will be able to stop the strikers, or the audience, from singing those songs. Nor should we. And if that happens, the police move in."

Hippie Havel jumped up, shaking his fist in the air, and shouted, "Then we will fight them!"

"No, we will *not* fight them," Reed replied. "Our goal is to put on a Pageant, not provoke a bloody riot at the Garden. That would serve no purpose."

"The standing army of the bourgeoisie cannot defeat thousands of workers fighting for their right to freedom of speech!" Havel exclaimed, standing in the middle of the seated group and still shaking his fist. "It'll be another free speech fight, the biggest ever!" He was referring to the IWW's famous free speech fights out West, where the IWW packed the jails of San Diego, Spokane, and other West Coast cities in their fights for the right to speak their dissenting views in public.

John Reed felt himself becoming angry with Havel. It was already too much pressure dealing with all the minutia of mounting the Pageant. He didn't need Hippie Havel adding more unwelcome pressure. "There's a better way to fight for our freedom of speech." He turned to Jessie Ashley, sitting with Margaret Sanger at the dining room table. "Jessie, we need you to go to court in the morning and get a judge to issue an injunction barring Sheriff Harburger from constraining our right to sing these songs."

Jessie nodded. "I'll do that, Jack."

"The courts belong to the bourgeoisie," Havel yelled. "We don't need ruling class judges to protect our rights! The workers must protect their own rights with their force of numbers!"

"There's no need to provoke a fight with the police when we don't need to," Reed said sternly. "Remember, the purpose of being at the Garden is to perform the Pageant, not battle the police."

"I say we vote on it," Havel replied.

"Hippie, you're an anarchist," Reed said. "You don't even believe in voting."

"I still say we vote on it!"

The pressure at last became too much for him, and Reed snapped. "Hippie, you're worse than useless, you're an obstacle to getting anything done. You muck things up at *The Masses* and every other group you're a part of. But I'm not going to put up with your nonsense here. Sit down and shut up. Jessie is going to court in the morning and getting an injunction against Sheriff Harburger's ban. There's not going to be any vote on that."

"Yes, I'm an anarchist," Hippie yelled, "and you're a damn dictator. No one put you in charge. You put yourself in charge because you're a goddamn Harvard boy, and you think that gives you the right to run things."

That was the final straw for Reed. "I think I have the right to run things because I know what needs to be done, and I know how to do it. Hippie, this isn't a meeting of *The Masses,* where you can say anything you want. This is a working meeting for the Pageant. If all you're going to do is yell and shake your fist, then get the hell out. Now, you sit down and shut up, or I'm throwing you out of this meeting."

"You have no authority to throw me out of this meeting," Hippie replied. "I can attend any meeting I want, and I can say anything I want."

Reed said nothing in reply. Instead, he strode through the crowd and grabbed Hippie Havel by the back of his collar and the seat of his pants and hustled him to the door. He opened the door and forced Havel out onto the landing. Then, with a heave, he tossed Havel down the stairs. Havel clattered down the stairs in a noisy tumble of arms and legs, landing in a heap at the bottom. He looked up at Reed glaring down at him from above and shook his fist up at him. "Reed, you're a goddamn bourgeois pig!"

"And you're a useless pain in the ass, Havel," Reed yelled back. "You show your ugly mug at these meetings again, and I'll throw your useless anarchist ass down these stairs again! Don't come back!" Then Reed stalked back into the meeting and slammed the door behind him. He glared in angry silence at the group inside.

Big Bill Haywood had sat impassively witnessing the confrontation during the entire ruckus. Now he spoke. "People say I have a reputation for violence. But I don't hold a candle to you Harvard boys."

That broke the tension. People laughed, and the group broke into loud applause.

Reed smiled. "OK, now let's get back to work. We've got a lot to do, and very little time in which to do it."

Mabel Dodge had hardly dared to breathe during the loud argument between Reed and Hippie Havel. Such angry and physical confrontations were outside her experience. Now she began breathing once again, and joined in the laughter and applause for John Reed. It had been a thrilling experience. She was glad she had witnessed it. And now she knew for sure that she was in love with John Reed.

The Firebrand of the Strike

The reporter for the New York *Globe* arrived in Paterson's Turn Hall just in time to witness the police attack the workers rehearsing the Pageant. Word had been circulating in New York's journalistic circles about the upcoming "IWW Pageant." The editors at the *Globe* thought there might be a good human interest story in the Paterson strikers rehearsing for the Pageant, so they dispatched the reporter to the scene. He took a train to Paterson and arrived in the packed Turn Hall just as 20 big men charged into a crowd of men and women and began beating them. The workers who jammed the hall unleashed a deafening chorus of hoots and boos at the men beating the strikers. It all looked like chaos to the reporter, a scene from the actual strike battle lines. Was it a rehearsal, or was it part of the strike?

"Are the police breaking up the rehearsal?" the reporter asked a booing worker next to him. The worker ceased booing and turned, smiling, to the reporter. "Police? Police, hell! They're just rehearsing the second act of the Pageant, that's all. It's when the police attack the picket lines. Those men you call the police are strikers themselves!"

"But, it looks so real," the reporter objected. "It looks like they're actually beating the strikers!"

The worker laughed. "They're just getting into their roles, that's all."

A woman worker standing on the other side of the reporter nudged him and said, "You want to see something? Look at this." She proudly rolled up her sleeve to reveal an ugly purple bruise on her arm. "I got that in rehearsal yesterday. You've got to make it look real."

The reporter whistled at the bruise, then asked, "Who's in charge of all this?"

The woman rolled down her sleeve and pointed to a young man down in front shouting directions at the strikers through a megaphone. "That's him," she said, "that's John Reed."

The reporter looked in the direction she pointed. John Reed was standing on a small stool yelling and gesturing at the strikers. His sleeves were rolled up and his shirt was stained with sweat from his exertions. "Good! Good!" he yelled through his megaphone. "Make it real! Make it real!" There were at least a thousand men and women in the hall, most on the floor, hundreds more hooting and hollering from the galleries above. The reporter couldn't tell if those were merely observers or participants. He turned to the woman who had displayed her bruised arm to him. "So, you're one of the performers?"

"I'm a performer, and I'm a striker," she replied.

"Are you afraid of getting stage fright when you get to Madison Square Garden?"

"I might be if I was pretending to be some fancy lady, but I'm not doing that. I'm just being myself. We're all just doing what we do every day on the picket lines." She laughed, "Why, we've already been performing the Pageant for over three months on the picket lines!"

"So, is this part of the strike, or is it the Pageant?"

"It's both, I suppose," the woman said. "The Pageant just tells what happened in the strike, so it doesn't make any difference. It's all the same. The Pageant is part of the strike, I guess."

The reporter smiled at that, and turned his attention back to the rehearsal. It went on for another hour or more. At the end, the raucous hall grew less noisy and he heard John Reed yell through his megaphone, "OK, now we sing the strike song I taught you!"

Reed began singing, and the workers in the hall gradually, haltingly, joined in as he led them in his song. The IWW was famous for singing, and the lyrics Reed sang were combative and uplifting, encouraging the listeners to fight on and never surrender. The reporter knew Reed had written lyrics as a student for Harvard's annual Hasty Pudding Club musical, and he began scribbling down the lyrics for Reed's new song in his notepad. Then stopped as he suddenly recognized the tune. Like John Reed, the reporter for the *Globe* had gone to Harvard. And, he realized, like Reed he had sung this song many times, although not with these particular lyrics. He smiled to himself. It was "Harvard, Old Harvard," a well-known school song. This will be a nice touch in the story, he thought, and scribbled in his notepad more furiously.

After the singing stopped, the workers all cheered, and then began filtering out of Turn Hall in a noisy jumble of laughing and talking. The *Globe* reporter made his way through the crowd of departing workers and found John Reed down front, discussing particulars with a young woman who seemed to be his assistant. He introduced himself, and asked for a few minutes to interview Reed about the Pageant rehearsals.

"Only if you interview my co-director first," Reed said, indicating the woman at his side. "She's doing as much directing as me, maybe more, because I can't be here all the time. She's also one of the picket captains, and has been to jail a dozen times already. She's going to be leading the strikers up Fifth Avenue to Madison Square Garden. She's the firebrand of the strike!"

The reporter looked at the young woman. She seemed to him to be more of a schoolgirl than a strike leader. "And who might you be?" he asked.

"I'm Hannah Silverman. I've never talked to a New York reporter before."

The reporter smiled. "Well, no need to be nervous, Miss Silverman. If you're the firebrand of the strike, perhaps it won't be the last time. How did you get involved in the strike?"

"I'm not nervous," Hannah replied. "I was just saying. And to answer your question, I worked in the Westerhoff silk mill. I went out on strike with everyone else. I march on the picket line at the Westerhoff every day. That's why the other workers made me the picket captain in charge of organizing the daily picketing, making sure we always have pickets on the line. That's why the police are always arresting me, to intimidate me and the others."

The reporter marveled at the young woman's words. Surely this mere wisp of a girl was exaggerating. "How old are you?" he asked.

"I'm 17-years-old," Hannah said.

The reporter stopped jotting in his notepad and looked at the girl. "Isn't that a bit young to be doing all that?"

Hannah Silverman seemed to draw herself up as she said, "I'm old enough to be a silk worker. I'm old enough to be a picket captain. And I'm old enough to go to jail."

"And what do your parents think of a nice Jewish girl like you going to jail?"

"My father also works in the Westerhoff mill," Hannah said. "He's also on strike. We walk the picket line together, and we go to jail together."

"So, your father approves of the strike and you being involved in it?"

"Of course he does, he's a worker, isn't he? And so am I. We're both workers in the same silk mill. Besides, there's a Jewish principle you've probably never heard of, but *goyim* should live by it, also. It's called *tikkun olam*, doing good deeds to make a better world. That's what we're all doing here, fighting for a better world."

The reporter wrote that down. Then he decided to change the subject. "How do the other workers, the Italian men, for instance, feel about being led by a Jewish girl?"

Hannah looked at the reporter for a moment. She started to say something, then thought better of it. Then she said, "It doesn't matter if you're a Catholic, a Protestant, or a Jew, and it doesn't matter if you're a man or a woman, we're all the same here, we're all workers, and we're all fighting for the same thing, for a better life for everyone. That's what the IWW believes, and that's what we all believe."

"What do you think about Big Bill Haywood bringing in the IWW to lead the strike?"

The question seemed to irk Hannah. "He's a good speaker, but he didn't bring in the IWW, and the IWW doesn't lead the strike. We workers in the mills are the IWW, and this is *our* strike, *we* lead the strike, and *we* brought in Big Bill Haywood, just as a speaker and adviser. Big Bill Haywood isn't getting beaten on the picket lines, we workers are. Did you see Big Bill Haywood get beaten up in rehearsal here today?"

"No," the reporter said, "but isn't the Pageant his idea?"

"Maybe the Pageant was his idea to begin with, but it's *our* Pageant now. We're the ones who've come up with the major scenes of the Pageant, not Big Bill Haywood. We're the ones who've suggested what songs we'll sing, not Big Bill Haywood. And we're the ones who are here rehearsing the Pageant every day. I don't see Big Bill Haywood anywhere around here, do you? This is *our* Pageant, telling the story of *our* strike, and I'm tired of always being asked about Big Bill Haywood."

The reporter quickly stammered an apology. "I'm sorry, Miss Silverman. I didn't mean to offend you. I'm just trying to understand what you think about the Pageant."

"This Pageant is as much a part of the strike as any picket line," Hannah said. "And we're going to take the strike to your New York City by means of this Pageant. That's why we're here every day rehearsing the Pageant. It's not a diversion from the strike; it's just another kind of strike work. And that is why I'm going to lead the march up Fifth Avenue past all the mansions of the bosses, and why I'm going to act in the Pageant once we get to Madison Square Garden. It's all part of the strike. The Pageant tells the truth about what is happening in Paterson more than any of your New York newspapers. Will you put *that* in your story?"

The reporter flipped his notepad closed and smiled at Hannah. "Yes, Miss Silverman, I will put it in my story, just the way you said it. You have my word." He offered his hand to the 17-year-old strike leader.

Hannah Silverman took his hand and shook it. Her grip was strong and firm.

A Forest of Fists

On May 28th, ten days before the scheduled June 7th date of the Pageant, the Executive Committee called a noon emergency meeting of all the Pageant's working committees. It was held at the Liberal Club above Polly's Restaurant on MacDougal Street. Perhaps 80 or 90 Village Bohemians, who comprised the working committee volunteers, were in attendance. A like number of Paterson silk workers who worked on the Pageant, led by Hannah Silverman, trekked the 15 miles from Paterson to attend. It had taken them over six hours to reach Greenwich Village. They had begun walking before dawn. At Hoboken, on the New Jersey side of the Hudson River, they had taken a ferry over to the Lackawanna Pier on the Manhattan side, and then walked up Christopher Street to the Village. It was the same route they would take on the day of the Pageant, only then they and their fellow Pageant participants would have a chartered train from Paterson to Hoboken.

The Club's large room was filled to capacity. The Paterson workers congregated toward the seats at the rear, deferring to the Villagers, who mostly took the chairs in the front. Carlo Tresca and Elizabeth Gurley Flynn sat, uncomfortably and toward the side, among the Villagers in the front row of chairs. The room was noisy with the buzz of conversation. People were asking each other why the Executive Committee had insisted that everyone attend who possibly could. Tresca, who's English was still rudimentary, sat silently, unsure of the words spoken around him. Flynn spoke to him softly from time to time, explaining the gist of the surrounding conversations. The noise of clanking dishes and utensils filtered up from Polly's Restaurant below. Hippolyte Havel could be heard insulting Polly's customers as he plopped their plates down in front of them.

At the front of the room the five members of the Pageant Executive Committee -- Big Bill Haywood, Jessie Ashley, Margaret Sanger, Mabel Dodge, and John Reed -- sat at a wooden table facing the audience. None of them looked happy. Big Bill sat at one end of the table facing the others at the table to his right. This was his habitual public posture. It was so he could present only his left profile to the audience and they would not see the drooping lid of his blind right eye. To Hannah Silverman, however, sitting toward the rear of the audience with her fellow Paterson silk workers, it seemed that Big Bill's entire face, indeed, his entire body, drooped. The strike had taken its physical toll on him. He hadn't been sleeping or eating much over the last few weeks. He'd lost much weight and his clothes hung on him as if a few sizes too large. He sat as if deflated, silently looking at the others at the table with him.

They, too, sat silent, waiting for the noise to die down. At the other end of the table sat John Reed, his head bowed, elbows resting on the table and his hands at his temples supporting his head. All the manic energy Hannah had witnessed since Reed first came to Paterson to take charge of Pageant rehearsals seemed to have dissipated. A great sadness seemed to envelope him. Mabel Dodge sat next to him. She looked straight ahead. As usual, her inscrutable face revealing nothing. Looking at the five grim figures sitting at the table, a feeling of foreboding came over Hannah.

Margaret Sanger, sitting in the middle of the group of five, rapped the wooden table with her knuckles and, in a loud voice, said, "Please, please, the meeting will come to order." The talking subsided and all waited expectantly for Sanger to continue. She looked down at the sheaf of papers she held, shuffled them nervously, and then looked up again at her audience.

"This meeting has been called to discuss the dire finances of the Pageant," she said. At that a buzz again arose from the audience. "Please, please," she said once again, "let me continue." The jumble of talking faded, and Sanger again looked at the papers in her hands. Then she spoke in a calm, business-like voice.

"This is a summary of the principal expenses for the Pageant already entailed or projected: Rental of the Garden for June 7th, $1,000; theatrical license, $250; erection of the special stage at the Garden, $600; scenery expenses, $600; program printing, $252; advertising just in the Socialist Party's newspaper, *The New York Call*, $275; chartering a special train to bring the Pageant performers from Paterson, and ferry transportation across the Hudson River, $681.28, our second largest expense."

At that point, Sanger's voice faltered and she put down the papers. She looked up again at her audience. "The list of expenses goes on. We intend to sell tickets for admission to the floor for $1.50 or $2 each, but the gallery seats will go for five, ten, or twenty-five cents each, as we want ordinary workers to be able to attend. However, it has become increasingly clear to the Executive Committee that we will be quite unable to meet all of the projected expenses. Even if we sell out the Garden, including all the floor seats, a major financial loss seems certain."

The room erupted into a chaos of noise. "What about asking for contributions?" someone asked.

"We have done that already, bringing in what we could," Sanger replied. She nodded to Mabel Dodge, sitting next to her. "Indeed, Mrs. Dodge has already paid the required $250 deposit on the Garden rental out of her own funds. If we cancel the Pageant, that deposit will be forfeited and she will lose her money. However, we will not be liable for the remaining $750 of the rental fee. In summary, in view of the enormous expenses of the Pageant, which we will not be able to recoup, the Executive Committee recommends that the Pageant be cancelled. This is a great disappointment to all of us on the Executive Committee, but we see no alternative."

Again the chaos of chatter broke out. In the midst of the noise, a sense of gloom settled over the room like a great gray blanket. The other members of the Executive Committee said nothing. Big Bill seemed to sag even more in his seat. John Reed didn't move, his head still in his hands, bowed in defeat. Margaret Sanger waited patiently for her announcement to sink in. Hannah Silverman turned quickly to her fellow Paterson workers and they fell into their own, separate, island of conversation, mouths working feverishly, hands gesticulating, heads nodding.

Then Elizabeth Gurley Flynn sprang to her feet and faced the audience. "Brothers and Sisters," she said, "this is not a defeat, this is all to the good! The Pageant would never have worked, in any case. It was overly ambitious, poorly planned, and doomed to fail." She waved her hand dismissively at the Village volunteers who sat around her. "It was just a fantasy of these Village amateurs, play acting at a strike."

"And if, somehow, it could have worked, it should not have worked. It would have been a distraction from the real work before us, that of winning the strike. The only way you can win a strike is through solidarity and direct action. You must picket, picket, and picket some more! Nothing must detract from that. The strike is on the verge of winning. All we need to do is maintain our solidarity and our pressure on the mill bosses.

It's now time to forget this silly play acting of the Pageant and get back to Paterson and win this strike!"

The members of the Executive Committee listened to Flynn in silence. At any other time, Big Bill would have argued with her. At any other time, John Reed would have jumped up to loudly disagree. Now, neither said a word, both discredited by their participation in the failed project. Their silence seemed to be an acknowledgment of the correctness of Flynn's harsh judgment of the Pageant.

Hannah Silverman, however, rose from the back of the room and tentatively raised her hand. "May I speak, please? I'm a Paterson silk worker, and I walked here from Paterson this morning with my fellow Paterson workers to attend this meeting." All eyes turned to Hannah as she gestured to the men and women who sat around her. Even John Reed came to life and finally lifted his bowed head to hear what his co-director had to say.

"My name is Hannah Silverman," she continued. "I have the greatest respect for Miss Flynn. She has helped organize many strikes all over this country, and has been arrested many times. I'm sure she knows far more about how to win a strike than I do. She has been a great inspiration to all of us in Paterson, including myself. I have learned to be more courageous by seeing her brave example. I do not have the experience of Miss Flynn of speaking in public, but I rise to respectfully disagree with Miss Flynn about the Pageant.

"Miss Flynn believes she knows best what the Paterson workers should be doing to win the strike. I'm just a young girl, just a mill worker, not a strike organizer, and the only strike I know is the Paterson strike. But, I have walked the picket lines in Paterson every day since the strike began. In fact, I am the picket captain for my mill, and I organize the picketing there. I have been beaten on the picket lines, and I have been arrested on the picket lines. As a Paterson mill worker who is out on the picket lines every day, rain or shine, I believe I know a little about how the Paterson workers feel about the Pageant.

"Since the beginning of the Pageant rehearsals I have also worked every day with Mr. Reed on the rehearsals, as have many of the men and women sitting here with me today. I have not seen Miss Flynn come to Turn Hall to watch even one of our rehearsals. Perhaps, then, she does not know what the Pageant is truly about, nor what the Pageant means to the silk workers of Paterson. Let me try to tell you what the Pageant means to us, and why the Pageant must go on.

"Miss Flynn says that the only way to win a strike is by picketing. I agree with her about the importance of picketing. But what is the purpose of a picket line? Isn't it to discourage scabs and stop them from crossing the picket line to work in the mills? But there are hardly any scabs in Paterson, and very few have tried to cross the picket lines since the strike began. That's because of the solidarity of all us workers in Paterson. Everyone supports the strike. Because of that, the mills are completely shut down, as tight as can be. More picketing will not shut them down any tighter than they are right now. Now, the only thing that happens on the picket line, and this is a daily occurrence, is that the police attack us, beat us, and jail us. We keep them busy.

"Also, there are 25,000 workers on strike in Paterson. Almost all of them have walked on the picket lines at one time or another. I know, because as a picket captain I help keep track of who is on the line, and who is not. But, with almost no one trying to cross the picket lines, we don't need 25,000 workers continually walking the lines day after day. Surely a thousand of them can be spared for the Pageant in order to take the strike to New York City?

"And that's what the Pageant is meant to do. It is not a distraction from the strike. It is a continuation of the strike, an expansion of the strike. By taking the strike to Madison Square Garden on Saturday, June 7th, we can be sure that everyone in New York will read about the Paterson strike the next day in their Sunday newspapers. We might even make the front pages. And if more people, more workers, know about our fight in Paterson, we will then get more financial support from their small contributions, and that will strengthen the strike and help us continue.

"So, the Pageant is not just some fantasy of these good hard-working Village people in this room with us, who are simply play acting about a strike. They have done much good work to make the Pageant happen, and we thank them for it. Perhaps the Pageant was their idea in the beginning. But the Pageant no longer belongs solely to them. The Pageant also belongs to us, the silk workers of Paterson. We have been working on the Pageant daily in Turn Hall for many days now, deciding on the scenes and rehearsing them. The Pageant is now *our* Pageant, and it belongs to us more than it belongs to the Executive Committee or anyone else, because it is the story of *our* lives, because it is telling about *our* fight.

"And we refuse to be silenced about our fight. We refuse to be treated like children, whose parents make the decisions for them. We will not allow anyone else to make our decisions for us. We will not let the Paterson bosses make decisions for us, we will not let the Executive Committee make decisions for us, and we will not let Miss Flynn make decisions for us. None of you know what is best for us. If the strike teaches us anything, it is that we must take control over our own lives, and not let others decide for us, and so we will make our own decisions about our own lives.

"So we have decided, right here today in this room, that the Pageant will go on, no matter what the Executive Committee decides. If the Executive Committee won't put on the Pageant, then we, the workers of Paterson, will put it on. We have just decided, right here today in this room, to raise the transportation expenses of the Pageant performers from Paterson to New York City. We are on strike and our families are hungry and starving. Even so, we will raise the money ourselves, with our own pennies and nickels and dimes out of our own nearly empty pockets, to pay the $681.28 you say is needed for that chartered train from Paterson. We will do this because we refuse to let the Paterson Pageant fail!"

At that, a chorus of loud assent burst forth from the workers around Hannah. As a body, the Paterson strikers rose and jammed their fists into the air, shouting their support. Raising her voice above the shouts of her fellow workers, Hannah said, "The Pageant is the story of the Paterson strike, and we Paterson strikers have decided that, one way or another, our story *will* be told. The Executive Committee will not be able to silence us, and even Miss Elizabeth Gurley Flynn will not be able to silence us!" She raised her fist above her head and shouted over the cheering of her fellow strikers, "Who will stand today in solidarity with the workers of Paterson?"

The volunteers on the various work committees jumped to their feet, shouting their solidarity, also jamming their fists into the air. John Reed rose to his feet, life coming back into him, and raised his fist as well, shouting along with everyone in else in the room. Big Bill Haywood rumbled to his feet and raised his fist in solidarity. Then Margaret Sanger, Jessie Ashley, and even Mabel Dodge, rose and thrust their fists into the air along with the Paterson workers. Only Carlo Tresca and Elizabeth Gurley Flynn did not join in the shouting, did not raise their fists in solidarity with the workers of

Paterson.

Big Bill looked directly at them with his one good eye. "Gurley, Carlo," he said amid the tumult. "We've stood together in every battle in this long hard strike. Don't abandon us now. Won't you stand in solidarity with us?"

The word, "solidarity," seemed to send an electric jolt through both Elizabeth Gurley Flynn and Carlo Tresca. They looked at each other, and then Carlo Tresca nodded, rose, smiled broadly, and thrust his fist into the air. Standing beside him, Elizabeth Gurley Flynn also raised her fist in solidarity. At that, the shouting of the people in the room became even louder and more raucous.

Hannah Silverman looked around the room. Everyone was standing and every fist was in the air, so that it looked like the room was a solid forest of fists. "Then it's unanimous!" she shouted jubilantly. "The Pageant goes on!"

Then she began a chant, which those in the room quickly took up, "All for one, and one for all! All for one, and one for all! All for one, and one for all!" The room seemed to shiver and shake with the stomping and cheering.

Downstairs, in Polly's restaurant, Hippolyte Havel looked up at the wooden beams supporting the ceiling. Dust, shaken loose by the shouting and stomping above, filtered down onto the restaurant's tables. He slapped the bowl of soup he was carrying down in front of his customer. "Here, you bourgeois pig," he said. "Eat your slop."

Then he turned and stalked silently back into the kitchen.

An Unlawful Assembly

Thursday, June 5th, dawned as yet another wet gray morning in Paterson. Still, as had been the case every morning since the strike began, Hannah Silverman and her pickets were parading at the main gate of the Westerhoff mill even before the sun rose. There was, as usual, little need for the 50 men and women to parade at the gate. There were no scabs trying to enter the mill. But, because Elizabeth Gurley Flynn and others insisted that picketing was how a strike was won, the striking workers picketed.

Hannah marched around and around in a big circle in front of the gate with the other pickets. Her mind, however, was elsewhere. She was preoccupied with thoughts about the Pageant rehearsal, which she and John Reed would oversee at Turn Hall later in the day. There were only two days of rehearsal left before the Pageant itself at Madison Square Garden on the upcoming Saturday. Hannah would have a leading role on the Garden stage as a picket captain, doing on stage exactly what she was doing now at the gates of the mill where she worked. It was a lot to think about.

Her thoughts were interrupted by the arrival of Chief of Police John Bimson at the head of a large contingent of his police, as well as many of the city's patrol wagons. Hannah was used to police harassment, but this level of police presence was unusual. Passersby stopped to watch in curiosity, and pickets from the other mill gates ceased their parading and began to drift over. Bimson's policemen quickly surrounded the fifty pickets that Hannah led. The pickets ceased their marching, standing in a clump facing the police who surrounded them.

Hannah approached Bimson and confronted him. "Chief Bimson, what is the meaning of this?"

"Well," he sneered, "if it isn't the little sheenie girl in charge of all the wops. I've been hearing a lot about you, Miss Silverman. It seems you're a big troublemaker for such a little slip of a girl."

"I asked the meaning of all this," Hannah replied, motioning to the ring of policemen surrounding her and her pickets.

Bimson's faced darkened and he frowned at Hannah. "You're an impudent little girl, aren't you, Miss Silverman? The meaning of all this is that you are leading an unlawful assembly. I am ordering you to disperse your pickets immediately. If you do not, you and all your pickets will be arrested!"

"We are peacefully picketing," Hannah replied. "We are within our rights, and we will not disperse."

Bimson smiled cruelly at the girl. "I was hoping you'd say that." He motioned to his men. "All right, boys, round them up!"

The policemen who stood at the back doors of the patrol wagons immediately swung open the doors while other policemen began hustling the pickets toward the wagons. Two burly policemen seized Hannah by her upper arms and lifted her easily. Hannah did not resist as they carried her to one of the patrol wagons and dumped her there. There was a tumult of pushing and shoving, but the pickets followed Hannah's example, and none resisted as the police herded them toward the patrol wagons. The crowd of hundreds who had gathered to witness the confrontation began booing and hooting noisily.

Hannah stood with her back to the open doors of the patrol wagon and raised her fist in defiance. "Solidarity forever!" she shouted, "solidarity forever!" The pickets being arrested with her raised their fists as well and shouted out after her, "Solidarity forever! Solidarity forever!" And then, as the police shoved them into the backs of the patrol wagons, they took it up as a singsong chant, "Solidarity forever! Solidarity forever!" Then the surrounding crowd of onlookers raised their fists and took up the chant, "Solidarity forever! Solidarity forever!"

The police shoved Hannah into the patrol wagon, already filled with other pickets, and slammed and locked the door. From inside the patrol wagon the crowd could still hear Hannah and her pickets chanting "Solidarity forever!" as the patrol wagons took off, clanging, down the street.

When she appeared before Recorder Carroll, he scowled down from his bench at the girl. "Hannah Silverman, you are a notorious law breaker," he said.

"Why, thank you, your honor," Hannah replied, and did a little curtsy.

Recorder Carroll glared at the girl. "That was not meant as a compliment, Miss Silverman. You have appeared before this court far too many times. You are still an underage minor, seventeen years of age. If you appear before this court one more time, I will sentence you to the State House for Girls in Trenton until the age of 21. Do you understand me, Miss Silverman?"

Hannah decided it would be wiser to keep her silence, and stifled the sarcastic reply that welled up inside her. She nodded silently.

"In the meantime, I am sentencing you to a fine of $60 or 60 days in the Passaic County Jail for leading an unlawful assembly." Recorder Carroll motioned to the two big policemen standing on either side of Hannah. "Take her away," he ordered.

The two policemen took Hannah to a cell in the police department to await transportation to the Passaic County Jail in the morning. The cells were already crowded with the 50 pickets who had been arrested for unlawful assembly along with her. When they saw Hannah, they erupted into cheers and applause. Hannah smiled at her reception and raised her fist in acknowledgement. The two big policemen who escorted her into the cellblock shoved her inside the cell, which was already jammed with female pickets, and slammed the door on her. They locked it and stalked away.

Hannah looked around at her cellmates. She knew every one of them. They were her pickets. "What did Recorder Carroll give you?" one of the women asked.

"Either $60 or 60 days," Hannah replied. "My family doesn't have $60, so I suppose I'll be spending the next 60 days as the county's guest."

There was a collective groan. "We all got $30 or 30 days," the woman said. "Why did you get 60?"

"Recorder Carroll said I was a notorious troublemaker. He wanted to teach me a lesson."

"Have you learned your lesson?"

Hannah smiled. "Not at all. If I've learned anything from this strike, it's how to be a troublemaker. I'll be a troublemaker until the day I die, and wherever I go, like right here in this cell. What do you say we start making some noise?"

With that, Hannah began clapping her hands. "Let's go, now," she said, "let's get it going!" The other women began clapping in unison along with Hannah, and then, as they clapped, Hannah began the singsong chant: "Solidarity forever! Solidarity forever!"

The women picked up the chant and began loudly chanting along with her as they clapped, "Solidarity forever! Solidarity forever!" The pickets jamming the other cells picked it up, and shortly the entire cellblock was clapping in unison and chanting, "Solidarity forever! Solidarity forever!"

Then Hannah led them in other raucous union and IWW songs, one after another, long into the night. They made it clear to the policemen listening in the rest of the station: Hannah's spirit wasn't broken by her confinement, and neither were the spirits of her fellow prisoners.

Eventually, Hannah let the chanting and singing die down. It was late, the day had been long, and they would need their rest for tomorrow when they would all be transported to the Passaic County Jail. Hannah didn't mind the 60-day sentence so much in itself. What saddened her was that she would not be able to participate in the Pageant that she'd worked so hard to rehearse. *It will still happen*, she told herself, as she lay in her bunk. *It is well rehearsed. Everybody knows their parts by heart. It will be magnificent, even without me. I just wish I could see it.* And then, still thinking of the Pageant, she drifted off.

Early the next morning a policeman clanged open her cell door and ordered her out. Resigned to her fate, Hannah obeyed him. As they exited the jail portion of the police station, Hannah saw Jessie Ashley, the elderly attorney for the IWW, and a member of the Pageant's Executive Committee, awaiting her. "Hannah!" Jessie said with a big smile, "You're free!"

Hannah was confused. "What do you mean, free?"

"We raised the money for your fine. You're free."

"What about the pickets who were arrested with me? What about their fines?"

Jessie Ashley sighed. "It was hard enough to raise the money for you, Hannah. We just don't have the money for more than one person."

"But, me? Why?"

"Why? Because we need you! You're the co-director of the Pageant. We need you at the Pageant. Besides, you have to lead the march of the strikers up Fifth Avenue tomorrow!"

"Anyone can do that."

"Yes, but we don't want just anyone to do that. We want Hannah Silverman to do that. You've become the heroine of the strike. Now, come with me, you're free!"

Hannah hesitated, not wanting to leave her fellow pickets behind. Jessie Ashley touched her arm, prodding her, and nodded toward the exit. Hannah finally nodded in response and, with Jessie Ashley leading the way, walked out of the police station into another gray day in Paterson.

A Better World in Birth

The next morning, Saturday, June 7th, around 1,500 strikers who would participate in the Pageant assembled at 8:00 o'clock in Paterson's Turn Hall. There, Hannah Silverman gave them their final instructions. Then, preceded by several bands comprised of strikers, she led them through the streets of Paterson to the train station. There, at 10:45, they boarded their chartered train, paid for by their own pennies and nickels and dimes. The train took them to Hoboken, on the Hudson River. Another 800, who were not part of the Pageant, set out after the train left on foot. They planned to walk the 15 miles from Paterson to New York in time for the Pageant's performance that night at Madison Square Garden.

At Hoboken the Pageant participants boarded ferries to cross the Hudson and bring them to Manhattan's Lackawanna Pier. There, a large IWW band awaited them. The strikers formed up into a long column with Hannah Silverman at their head. Hannah wore a white linen dress with a large red sash draped diagonally across her torso, as did many of the other women strikers. Written on the sash, in white, were large letters spelling out, "I.W.W." American flags, which strikers all down the column carried, surrounded her. The flags proclaimed that these immigrant workers, all of them, Poles, Jews, Italians, all of them, were American workers.

And then, led by the IWW band and a police vanguard that cleared the way along the parade route, the column of strikers set out for the long march through the city to Madison Square Garden. All along their route massive crowds of gawking men, women, and children lined the streets to catch a sight of the marching strikers. For these thousands of New Yorkers, the Pageant performance was already underway, and they were watching it.

Alternately singing *The Marseillaise* and *The Internationale*, the Paterson strikers marched up the length of Christopher Street, then turned right to march along the northern edge of Washington Square. They marched past the Washington Square Arch, atop which John Reed and his fellow Bohemians had proclaimed the independent Republic of Greenwich Village only six months before. At that time, John Reed had hoped for a real revolution. Now, it seemed, that real revolution was marching in the streets below the Washington Arch.

The marching column turned left and began its insurrectionary parade up posh Fifth Avenue. The strikers passed the Brevoort Hotel on their left, where the literati met to socialize. They passed Mabel Dodge's brownstone on their right, where some among them had argued with artists and writers about the strike. They marched past the triangular Flat Iron Building, many of them seeing it for the first time, and then they reached Madison Square Park itself.

Just after 1870, Ignatz Pilat, an associate of Central Park creator Frederick Law Olmsted, had designed Madison Square Park, with its winding paths and spouting fountains. It was the center of the wealthiest residential neighborhood in New York City. Bordered by 23rd and 26th Streets to the south and north, and by Fifth Avenue, Broadway, and Madison Avenue to the west and east, it was the park of New York society's *crème de la crème*. Theodore Roosevelt and Edith Wharton grew up in the surrounding neighborhood and Wharton described it in her novel, *The Age of Innocence*. Mark Twain and O. Henry had strolled through the park after dining at one of the nearby fancy restaurants. In 1876, at the southwest corner of the park at Fifth Avenue and 23rd Street, a grateful nation had erected a statue of William H. Seward. He was the Secretary of State under Presidents Lincoln and Andrew Johnson who had finagled the purchase of Alaska from Russia in 1867. In the southeast corner of the park stood a statue erected in 1893 of Roscoe Conkling, the U. S. Senator and Republican Party power broker. He had collapsed and died at that spot when caught in the great blizzard of 1888.

On the eastern edge of the park was the prestigious Madison Square Presbyterian Church, an impressive structure combining Corinthian columns at the entrance with a dome inspired by Istanbul's Hagia Sofia. On the western edge of the park stood the magnificent Fifth Avenue Hotel, built just before the Civil War in 1859. It boasted over 600 rooms and the first hotel passenger elevator in America. It was a gathering place for the moneyed classes and the political, artistic, and financial elites of the nation. Mark Twain and the actor Edwin Booth stayed there when in town. Gilded Age Robber Barons like Jay Gould and Jim Fisk had plotted their takeovers there. A bench in the hotel's lobby, known as the "Amen Corner," was famous as a place where Republican political bosses planned strategy. Every American president from James Buchanan to William McKinley stayed at the Fifth Avenue Hotel.

And at the northeastern corner of the park stood Madison Square Garden Theatre, boasting the largest arena and stage in New York City. It was the site of many rallies for politicians and even presidents. When P. T. Barnum brought his circus to town, it performed at the Garden. When Buffalo Bill brought his Wild West Show to New York, his cowboys and Indians staged their mock battles at the Garden.

Now the marching Paterson strikers, with Hannah Silverman at their head, marched up to Stanford White's grand edifice. On all four sides of the looming tower where White had once cavorted with the teenage Evelyn Nesbit, electric signs composed of ten-foot tall letters spelled out, "I.W.W." These letters were constructed of large red bulbs. Once night fell they would be turned on and the initials would blaze out luridly over all of Manhattan, proclaiming the presence of the radical union in one of the famous palaces of the ruling class. The marching strikers reached the Garden, and passed inside.

Inside the Garden they found an enormous amphitheater, 188-feet by 304-feet, with a high roof of exposed steel beams. The space was big enough to be used for many purposes, including sporting events, circuses, and races. Indeed, just shortly before the Pageant, the National Horse Show had taken place at the Garden, with hundreds of horses and buggies parading around inside.

Or, it could be used for theatrical spectacles, such as the Pageant. John Sloan and his crew had worked hard on the city block-long stage, big enough to accommodate all of the Pageant participants simultaneously. The 200-foot long painted backdrop portrayed a gigantic silk mill, with smaller mills flanking the sides. The black curtain entrance to the mill was wide enough to allow 30 workers at a time to enter its gaping maw. The entire image was backlit with powerful lights, which made the many tiers of windows glow with a demonic ferocity. It was the very emblem of a dark satanic mill.

Leading from the Garden entrance up to the stage was a wide aisle, as wide as a road, by which the Pageant participants would enter and leave the stage. It had the effect of also making the entire floor audience participants in the Pageant, either as witnesses to a parade of workers, or as an audience actually attending the events portrayed in the

Pageant. Above the floor were many tiers of galleries, which would shortly be filled with a working class audience. And everywhere in the hall were red banners and IWW flags and banners emblazoned with militant slogans.

Once the column of marchers entered the building, John Reed and Hannah Silverman, megaphones in hand, assembled and led the workers through one last rehearsal on the stage that John Sloan had constructed, and which the strikers were seeing for the first time. Then Margaret Sanger and a small army of volunteers from the various Pageant work committees set out many tables laden with sandwiches. The hungry strikers fell upon the food like a ravening horde.

And, while they ate, John Reed retreated to the makeshift office he had made for himself in one of the rooms of Stanford White's proud tower. There, he collapsed in a chair. He had done all he could on the Pageant, from conception to final rehearsal. It had been a three-week roller coaster of frantic activity, great anxieties, and intense emotions. He had doubted many times that the Pageant would actually happen. Now, it was out of his hands, and would soon be over. It was a huge behemoth proceeding under its own momentum. Whether it was a success or a failure, it had gone beyond him.

A great exhaustion suddenly overwhelmed him. It had always seemed that he had more manic energy than his body could possibly contain, an inexhaustible supply of stamina and enthusiasm. Now he felt drained. He sagged listlessly in his chair and listened to the dull roar of the thousands of workers below him in the amphitheater, eating, shouting, and cheering. Despite the noise, he felt he could barely stay awake. He had hardly slept at all for the last three weeks. Day and night he had worked on the Pageant. How tiring it had been!

And then doubts about it all flooded in on him. He suddenly wondered, what the hell were we all thinking? None of us are theater professionals. We hardly know what we're doing. No one who will be on that stage is an actor. They're all just mill hands. It's going to be a huge disaster. Tomorrow morning all the critics for the big newspapers will crucify us, laugh at us amateurs for trying to pull off something like this. Put more than a thousand mill hands on the biggest stage in New York? Portray an entire three-month strike on stage in just a few hours? Maybe Gurley Flynn was right, the whole thing is crazy. It's overly ambitious, chaotically planned, and lacking in resources. We're going to loose our shirts on it, that's for sure. I wanted to tell the story of those proud people I met in the jail. Maybe I aimed too high. Maybe I should have been content with just writing the article for *The Masses*. Maybe it's all just hubris, and I was a fool. John Reed buried his face in his arms on the desk in front of him and apologized internally to the workers of Paterson for having led them astray in such a horrible way.

It was in that position that Mabel Dodge found him. "Reed," she said, "what's wrong? Everybody is looking for you. Why are you hiding up here?"

John Reed raised his head and looked at her. Mabel was shocked at his bloodshot eyes and haggard face. "John, what is it?"

"It's all going to be a fiasco, Mabel. I'm such a failure. Why did I ever think we could mount a Pageant of the strike here in Madison Square Garden? I got carried away. Why the hell did I ever think Village Bohemians and Paterson workers could ever come together? What the hell do they even have in common?"

Mabel was shocked at Reed's words. She had never known John Reed to falter in this manner. His energy and enthusiasm were legendary. He had always insisted that the impossible could be done, and that he and those around him were the ones who could do it. His determination about that had always inspired those around him to also believe the impossible could be done. He brought them all together, regardless of differences, and gave them the courage to strive for a common goal, utopian though it might seem to all others. That's what had drawn Mabel to him. And now he was faltering, just on the cusp of victory. Mabel could hardly believe it.

"John Reed," she said, "I have no idea what you are talking about! You are not a failure! The Pageant is not a failure! We are not failures! We have done what no one said could be done. No one thought it was possible, but we have brought the strike to New York City. We have invented a new type of theater. This is the first genuine labor play in the history of America! It's not a theater of actors playing at their roles. It's not actors play-acting at a strike. That's the whole point! It is part of the strike itself, performed by the strikers themselves, performed for other workers just like themselves.

"No one has ever seen anything like this in the history of theater, Jack. And we did it! We made it happen! There are thousands of people downstairs who would not be there but for you. Many thousands more, Bohemians and ordinary workers and socialists and Wobblies, will be in the audience tonight joining those thousands on stage. No one thought it was possible for all those different kinds of people to come together.

"And all those thousands are going to go home tonight with new hope in their hearts because of what they saw and heard and experienced tonight. What do they all have in common, you ask? Hope that there's a better world for all of us, Jack. And it's all because of you! You can't give up now! You can collapse all you want after tonight. But right now, there are thousands of people downstairs calling for you. So, buck up, and come downstairs, and join the strike!"

John Reed listened to what Mabel Dodge said in astonishment. He had never known her to speak at such length, or with such vehemence. Something seemed to have changed in her. It seemed that she believed in what she was saying in a way she had never believed in anything before. It seemed that she actually believed that it was possible to change the world and make it better, and that she and John Reed and the thousands of strange and disparate people downstairs were the ones who were going to do it.

John Reed rose from his chair and took Mabel's face in his hands. He looked into her eyes. "You're damn right, Mabel. We're going to change the world tonight! And we're going to do it together!" And then he kissed her, fiercely and passionately.

Surprised, Mabel stiffened for a moment. Then she put her arms around John Reed and kissed him just as fiercely and passionately.

****

By 8:30 P.M. twilight was falling over New York City. On Stanford White's tall tower the red electric letters of the IWW beamed their light out over the city. Inside, Madison Square Garden was jammed to capacity with more than 15,000 shouting, cheering, singing workers, Bohemians, Socialists, Wobblies, and riff-raff. The galleries were filled, the floor was filled, and people were pushed up against the walls. The vast cavern rocked with noise. The galleries, where seats went for a few pennies, had filled first. Finally, people were allowed onto the more expensive floor spaces for anything they could pay. Many waved their IWW membership cards, and were allowed in for free. The 800 Paterson strikers who had walked all the way from Paterson were allowed in for free. New York silk workers who were also on strike were allowed in for free. It was clear that the Pageant was going to be a financial loss, but thousands of New Yorkers were nevertheless going to see it.

Outside, many thousands more clamored for entrance. The massive crowd spilled out over Madison Square Park and spread for blocks around. Sheriff Julius Harburger was on hand with a large contingent of his officers. They struggled to bring some kind of order out of the surging crowd. In the meantime, he vented his opinion of the IWW to the reporters surrounding him, eagerly writing down his words. The Pageant, he fumed, was certain to contain, "sedition, treasonable utterances, un-American doctrines advocating sabotage, inflammatory, hysterical, unsound doctrines." A court order had forbidden him from preventing the singing of *The Marseillaise* and *The Internationale*, but, he swore, if the strikers uttered one single word of disrespect for the American flag, "I'll shut down this show so fast it will take your breath away!"

At 9:00 P.M. the doors were closed, leaving many thousands who could not gain entrance outside. The amphitheater lights dimmed, leaving the backlit drop of the gigantic mill on stage glowing like a huge demonic Moloch, and the performance began. From behind the backdrop of the mill came the sound of thunderous clanging and booming, as if the gods themselves were hammering on their forges.

Spotlights overhead came on to illuminate only the path down the middle of the audience. Then, from the back of the hall, the long column of workers entered, plodding slowly to work, heads down, shoulders slumped, collars turned up against the chill of the February morning when the strike began. The audience watched in silence as the workers slowly climbed the stairs to the stage and entered the black maw of the clanging factory. The last of them finally disappeared inside as the pounding of the machinery continued, as if grinding up the very bodies of the workers.

And then the machines stopped, the pounding ceased, and silence filled the hall. And then the workers, a thousand and more of them, erupted from the gaping maw of the factory with Hannah Silverman in their lead, all shouting and cheering and leaping in joy. The strike was on! They sang and danced and laughed, and the thousands in the audience burst into thunderous applause.

And then the workers on stage raised their fists and a thousand and more voices began chanting Strike! Strike! Strike! The thousands in the audience took up the chant, and the interior of Madison Square Garden boomed with the mighty roar of Strike! Strike! Strike! Suddenly, the police, those in the Pageant, charged the strikers, beating and pummeling them in a wild chaotic melee, with Hannah Silverman being singled out for particular attention. Shots rang out on stage, and a striker fell to the floorboards, the killing of Valentino Modestino. The chaos eventually resolved itself into some kind of order as the Pageant police dragged Hannah and a few hundred other strikers off the stage and down the center aisle toward the back.

The remaining strikers on stage hooted and booed the police, and the many thousands in the audience joined in the verbal abuse hurled at the police in one long chronic cyclone of sound. All were on their feet, and all remained on their feet for the rest of the performance. The lights died down, and the IWW orchestra, in the pit in front of the stage, segued into a mournful death march.

Finally, from the back of the hall, a column of workers slowly entered. At the head of the column the workers carried a coffin, that of Modestino. The audience became the people of Paterson, lining the street to witness the funeral procession carrying Modestino's coffin to the cemetery. His widow had been given a reserved box seat above and to the right of the stage. As she caught sight of her husband's coffin, she broke into loud hysterical sobs. Many in the audience then began sobbing with her.

Watching the procession from the audience, Mabel Dodge felt that, for a few electric moments, there was a terrible unity between everyone in the vast hall. The line between performers and spectators was breached. They were all one, she felt: the workers in the audience, and the workers marching with the coffin, everyone. Never in her life had Mabel felt such a high pulsing vibration in any gathering. She, too, became one with the workers. She glanced at John Reed standing next to her. Tears were streaming down his face. He, too, felt the terrible unity of the night.

The column of workers carried the coffin up to the stage, where Elizabeth Gurley Flynn, Carlo Tresca, and Big Bill Haywood solemnly awaited them. The funeral procession placed the coffin in front of them, and then stepped back. Elizabeth Gurley Flynn, Carlo Tresca, and Big Bill Haywood then delivered the same eulogies they had given at the actual funeral of Modestino. It was if Valentino Modestino was being buried a second time, with the 15,000 workers in the audience now in attendance at the funeral.

Speaking wholly in Italian, perhaps unintelligible to the English speakers, Carlo Tresca promised blood for blood, *sangue per sangue*. The three IWW speakers were now speaking to all the many thousands in the audience, who were now no longer an audience observing the events on the stage, but melded solidly with the performers as one vast congregation. Class-consciousness became no mere abstraction. They were all experiencing it.

When Big Bill Haywood finished his eulogy, the thousand and more workers on stage filed past the coffin, each dropping a red carnation upon the casket. Soon, a huge red mound, the color of blood, covered the entire casket. And then the workers on stage, and the many thousands of workers in the audience, all sang *The Marseillaise* in a thundering and defiant chorus.

And so it went, scene after scene, as the performers on stage reenacted the major events of the Paterson strike, and the huge audience of workers seemed to participate in every scene along with them. That night, every one of them was a Paterson worker, every one of them marched, and struggled, and endured with the strikers.

The last scene of the Pageant was a recreated strike meeting. Big Bill Haywood stood on a platform with his back to the mill, facing outward to the Paterson strikers gathered around him on stage, facing outward to the thousands in the vast arena, who thereby also became participants in one gigantic strike meeting.

"Sister and brother workers," Big Bill said in a stentorian voice that filled the hall, "you are the workers of all the world. You are more important to society than any judge, lawyer, politician, or capitalist – or any man who does not work for an honest living. You came to America with the expectation of improving your conditions. You expected to find the land of the free. But you found that we of America were but economic slaves as you were in your homeland. I extend to you the hand of brotherhood with no thought of nationality. The Boss can lick one Pole. The Boss can lick one Jew. The Boss can lick one Italian. In fact, the Boss can lick all the Poles. The Boss can lick all the Jews. The Boss can lick all the Italians.

"But the Boss cannot lick all the nationalities of all the workers when they fight together. There are no immigrants here tonight. We are all Americans here tonight! There is no foreigner here among us tonight but the capitalist Boss. It doesn't matter where you come from, or what you look like, or what language you speak. All that matters is what you believe, what values you hold dear. Do not let the Boss divide you by sex, color, creed, or nationality. The IWW is composed of all different nationalities, all different races, all different religions, all different vocations, all fighting together for a better world. And with such a fighting force you can lick the Boss! As you stand here tonight, united as one, you are invincible." And with that, Big Bill raised his big fist and shook it threateningly in the air.

And all the strikers on stage raised their fists and began chanting, Strike! Strike! Strike! And everyone in the vast hall, those jammed together on the floor, those packing the galleries above, everyone raised their fists and took up the chant, Strike! Strike! Strike! Those in the galleries began stomping their feet, and the galleries shook as if they would collapse. The many thousands still waiting outside heard the chants and they, too, took it up, Strike! Strike! Strike!

And then, from the wings, John Reed strode on stage to stand beside Hannah Silverman, chanting in the midst of the crowd. He raised his fist along with her. They stood together and together they chanted, Strike! Strike! Strike! John Reed looked out over the thousands of people jammed into the auditorium and thought to himself, no matter what happens next, whether we win or lose the strike, these are the people who will change the world. Then he corrected himself: *We* are the people who will change the world! It's beautiful! It's frightening! It's magnificent!

The thousands in the audience began weeping as they applauded and stomped their feet. The events on stage in the pageant had been as real to them as their very own lives. They wept for themselves. They cheered for themselves. And those on stage and those in the audience melded into one overwhelming soul shaking religious communion.

And then they all began singing, Hannah Silverman and John Reed, Mabel Dodge and Margaret Sanger, Big Bill Haywood, Carlo Tresca, and Elizabeth Gurley Flynn, the Paterson strikers on the stage, the New York workers filling the hall, and the Village Bohemians and Socialists and Wobblies and riff-raff who stood amongst them, all singing as one.

And, from outside, they could hear the thousands of workers who jammed Madison Square Park joining in the singing. They were all, all of them, singing *The Internationale*:

> "Arise, ye prisoners of starvation,
> Arise, ye wretched of the Earth,
> The Earth shall rise on new foundations,
> A better world's in birth."

About the Author:

Eric Leif Davin, Ph.D., is the author of *The Great Strike of 1877: A Novel, Crucible of Freedom: Workers' Democracy in the Industrial Heartland, 1914-1960,* and *Radicals in Power: The New Left Experience in Office.*

Lightning Source UK Ltd.
Milton Keynes UK
UKHW012242131220
375115UK00001B/23